MATH PHONICS™

MULTIPLICATION

&

DIVISION

BONUS BOOK–ALL NEW IDEAS

Quick Tips and Alternative
Techniques for Math Mastery

BY MARILYN B. HEIN

ILLUSTRATED BY RON WHEELER

Teaching & Learning Company

1204 Buchanan St., P.O. Box 10
Carthage, IL 62321-0010

j372.7
HEI

THIS BOOK BELONGS TO

_____

ACKNOWLEDGEMENTS

Mary Gallagher and Jed and Todd Shepherd and Amy McEachern for tech support.

DEDICATION

To those who died September 11, 2001. They taught us lessons never found in books.

Cover art by Ron Wheeler

Copyright © 2002, Teaching & Learning Company

ISBN No. 1-57310-346-2

Printing No. 987654321

Teaching & Learning Company
1204 Buchanan St., P.O. Box 10
Carthage, IL 62321-0010

The purchase of this book entitles teachers to make copies for use in their individual classrooms only. This book, or any part of it, may not be reproduced in any form for any other purposes without prior written permission from the Teaching & Learning Company. It is strictly prohibited to reproduce any part of this book for an entire school or school district, or for commercial resale.

All rights reserved. Printed in the United States of America.

Math Phonics™ is a registered trademark to Marilyn B. Hein.

TLC10346 Copyright © Teaching & Learning Company, Carthage, IL 62321-0010

TABLE OF CONTENTS

Dear Teacher or Parent,

Hear it! See it! Touch it! Say it! Write it! Learn it!

That's how Math Phonics™ works. It uses the ears, eyes, fingers, voice and pencil to help students understand and master basic mathematics. If I could figure out a way to help them sniff out the answers, I would put that in this book, too!

This *Math Phonics™—Multiplication & Division Bonus Book* builds on the original multiplication and division books. If you haven't purchased and used them, please do. They contain many excellent ideas which are not repeated in this book. This bonus book focuses on harder basic facts and more advanced problems and has new demonstrations, activity pages, worksheets and even a new format for flash cards and fact charts.

Some concepts and skills are taught by means of games and puzzles. Teacher Amy McEachern said the other teachers in her building could tell something unusual was going on in her room. They asked her how in the world she got her students excited about learning the multiplication facts. She showed them her "math bible," her Math Phonics™ book!

I have invested thousands of hours into the development of the Math Phonics™ series. Why? Because I am frustrated at the number of people who say they hated math when they were young. I think we can do better.

The teachers in the adult education center near my home use *Math Phonics™* books with their students. My friend, Sue Wilkey, has told me that on many occasions she has shown someone the Math Phonics™ memory tricks for multiplication. The person stares at the paper for a minute and then says, "Why didn't someone show me this a long time ago?"

Please take a look at Math Phonics™ and please show it to your students!

Sincerely,

Marilyn

Marilyn B. Hein

TLC10346 Copyright © Teaching & Learning Company, Carthage, IL 62321-0010

WHAT IS MATH PHONICS™?

Math Phonics™ is a specially designed program for teaching multiplication and division facts initially or for remedial work.

WHY IS IT CALLED MATH PHONICS™?

In reading, phonics is used to group similar words, and it teaches the students simple rules for pronouncing each word.

In *Math Phonics™*, math facts are grouped and learned by means of simple patterns, rules and mnemonic devices.

In reading, phonics develops mastery by repetitive use of words already learned.

Math Phonics™ uses drill and review to reinforce students' understanding.

HOW WAS MATH PHONICS™ DEVELOPED?

Why did "Johnny" have so much trouble learning to read during the years that phonics was dropped from the curriculum of many schools in this country? For the most part, he had to simply memorize every single word in order to learn to read, an overwhelming task for a young child. If he had an excellent memory or a knack for noticing patterns in words, he had an easier time of it. If he lacked those skills, learning to read was a nightmare, often ending in failure–failure to learn to read and failure in school.

Phonics seems to help many children learn to read more easily. Why? When a young child learns one phonics rule, that one rule unlocks the pronunciation of dozens or even hundreds of words. It also provides the key to parts of many larger words. The trend in U.S. schools today seems to be to include phonics in the curriculum because of the value of that particular system of learning.

As a substitute teacher, I have noticed that math teacher manuals sometimes have some valuable phonics-like memory tools for teachers to share with students to help them memorize math facts–the addition, subtraction, multiplication and division facts which are the building blocks of arithmetic. However, much of what I remembered from my own education was not contained in the available materials. I decided to create my own materials based upon what I had learned during the past 40 years as a student, teacher and parent.

The name *Math Phonics™* occurred to me because the rules, patterns and memory techniques that I have assembled are similar to language arts phonics in several ways. Most of these rules are short and easy to learn. Children are taught to look for patterns and use them as "crutches" for coming up with the answer quickly. Some groups have similarities so that learning one group makes it easier to learn another. Last of all, *Math Phonics™* relies on lots of drill and review, just as language arts phonics does.

Children *must* master addition, subtraction, multiplication and division facts and the sooner the better. When I taught seventh and eighth grade math over 20 years ago, I was amazed at the number of students who had not mastered the basic math facts. At that time, I had no idea how to help them. My college math classes did not give me any preparation for that situation. I had not yet delved into my personal memory bank to try to remember how I had mastered those facts.

When my six children had problems in that area, I was strongly motivated to give some serious thought to the topic. I knew my children had to master math facts, and I needed to come up with additional ways to help them. For kids to progress past the lower grades without a thorough knowledge of those facts would be like trying to learn to read without knowing the alphabet.

I have always marveled at the large number of people who tell me that they "hated math" when they were kids. I wonder how many of them struggled with the basic math facts when they needed to have them clearly in mind. I firmly believe that a widespread use of *Math Phonics*™ could be a tremendous help in solving the problem of "math phobia."

WHAT ARE THE PRINCIPLES OF MATH PHONICS™?

There are three underlying principles of *Math Phonics*™.

They are: 1. Understanding
2. Learning
3. Mastery

Here is a brief explanation of the meaning of these principles.

1. **UNDERSTANDING:** All true mathematical concepts are abstract which means they can't be touched. They exist in the mind. For most of us, understanding such concepts is much easier if they can be related to something in the real world—something that can be touched.

Thus I encourage teachers and parents to have students find answers for themselves using small objects, number lines and counting charts. I think this helps the students to remember answers once they have discovered them on their own.

Next we use the base 10 counting cart as a short cut to the same answer. If a child has seen the multiplication facts demonstrated by use of objects or the counting chart, she is much more likely to learn and master them.

2. **LEARNING:** Here is where the rules and patterns mentioned earlier play an important part. A child can be taught a simple rule and on the basis of that, call to mind a whole set of math facts. But the learning necessary for the addition, subtraction, multiplication and division facts must be firmly in place so that the information will be remembered next week, next month and several years from now. That brings us to the next principle.

3. **MASTERY:** We have all had the experience of memorizing some information for a test or quiz tomorrow and then promptly forgetting most of it. This type of memorization will not work for the math facts. In order for children to master these facts, *Math Phonics*™ provides visual illustrations, wall charts, flash cards, practice sheets, worksheets and games. Some students may only need one or two of these materials, but there are plenty from which to choose for those who need more.

TLC10346 Copyright © Teaching & Learning Company, Carthage, IL 62321-0010

HOW TO MAKE A FLIP FOLDER

Flip folders are great for studying groups of multiplication or division facts. Put one group of facts on each page—2s through 9s, or use the top page as a title page and do 3s through 9s. They can also be used for studying other groups of information.

MATERIALS: 4 sheets of 8½" x 11" paper—white or 4 different colors, stapler

DIRECTIONS: Draw a dotted line on each sheet of paper as shown.

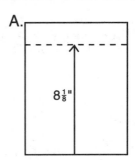
A.
$8\frac{1}{8}$"

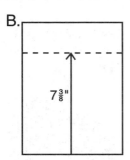
B.
$7\frac{3}{8}$"

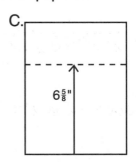
C.
$6\frac{5}{8}$"

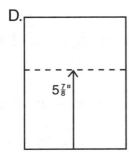
D.
$5\frac{7}{8}$"

Fold each page on the dotted line.

Page D slips inside page C, both slip inside B and all three slip inside A.

The four pages form an eight-page flip folder.

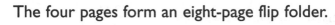

Lift up the top four pages and staple four times just below the fold.

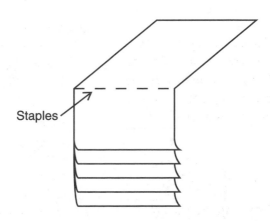
Staples

SUMMARY OF THE 10 BASIC STEPS

1. Demonstrate the Basic Concept of Multiplication

This step shows how to present the concept of multiplication to a class which has never multiplied before, or to refresh the student's understanding if this is a second time around. Students will practice on zeros, ones, twos and tens.

2. 5s, 9s & Squares

This step has ways of teaching these groups which were not given in the original *Math Phonics™–Multiplication* book. Materials in both books can be interchanged.

3. 3s & 4s

Once again, all new techniques.

4. 6s, 7s & 8s

As before, these groups are presented with all new materials. This lesson plan contains an original game which students should enjoy.

5. Three-Way Flash Cards

This is the transition step between multiplication and division. The flash cards can be used to study both processes.

6. Division for Squares & 9s

In this step, students learn to use the multiplication mini facts chart to find division answers. Dividends and divisors in this step are larger than basic math facts.

7. Division for 2s, 4s & 8s

This step contains a logic game to help students develop the more complex thought processes.

8. Division for 3s & 6s

This step contains a mental math trick, predict the answer, for students to try on friends or relatives. Here students begin to work with remainders.

9. Division for 5s & 7s

More practice—new techniques. Ideas for classroom card games.

10. Rules, Games & Assessments

This step contains a reference page for looking up rules, the games in this book and assessments in this book and others.

TLC10346 Copyright © Teaching & Learning Company, Carthage, IL 62321-0010

LESSON PLAN 1: BASIC CONCEPT OF MULTIPLICATION

OBJECTIVE: Teach or review the basic idea of multiplication, a shortcut to adding the same number several times. Also, briefly cover 0s, 1s, 2s and 10s.

NOTE: Those groups are taught on pages 42-53 of *Math Phonics™–Multiplication*, and are usually fairly easy to learn. Many helpful memory tricks are given in that book. Refer to that book if students need help with those groups.

MATERIALS: activity page—Groups of 7 (page 11), overhead projector markers and page protectors (optional), Base 10 Counting Charts (page 12), Basic Facts Charts (page 13), worksheets (pages 14-17)

DEMONSTRATION:

1. Use page 11, Groups of Seven. (Sevens will be taught in detail in Lesson Plan 4. To reinforce them, we use them as an example here, also. Sevens are hardest for many students.)

2. Explain that 1 x 7 means 1 written 7 times and added, or one row of desks with seven in that row.

3. Have students write in the numbers 1 through 7 in the first row of boxes (think of them as desks) and in the blank, write 1 x 7 = 7.

4. In row two, they continue numbering the boxes 8 through 14 and write 14 in the blank for 2 x 7.

5. Point out that 2 x 7 is the same as the doubles for addition 7 + 7, two rows of desks with 7 in each row.

$$\begin{array}{r} 7 \\ + 7 \\ \hline 14 \end{array} \qquad 2 \times 7 = 14$$

6. Continue having them number the boxes and fill in the answers to the 7s multiplication facts.

7. Point out to them that the first four and a half rows are like a calendar. They can look at a calendar at the 7 and the first three numbers under it for the first four answers in the sevens.

$$7 \times 1 = 7$$
$$7 \times 2 = 14$$
$$7 \times 3 = 21$$
$$7 \times 4 = 28$$

If some students need more help, use ideas on page 10 in *Math Phonics™–Multiplication* (hereafter referred to as MPM).

HANDOUT: Give each student a copy of page 12, containing four base 10 counting charts. To re-use the charts, give each student a vinyl page protector and overhead projector pen. Have them count 7 numbers and circle the 7, count 7 more and circle the 14 and so on. Use these for 2s and 10s and with later lesson plans in this book.

CLASSROOM DRILL: Have the class chant the 0s, 1s, 2s and 10s in unison. Also, have them chant the 7s. For those who need visual reinforcement, run off page 13 for a classroom poster or use it with the overhead projector.

WORKSHEETS: Students can do Worksheet A and then quiz each other verbally using the worksheet as a guide.

For Worksheet B, demonstrate 20 x 2. This is the same as 20 + 20 = 40. Also, think of 20 as 2 dimes and zero pennies. When you multiply 2 x 0 you get 0 in the 1s place for the pennies. 2 x 2 gives 4 dimes—put it in the 10s place. For 2 x 200, multiply the non-zero numerals and add as many zeros to the answer as there are in the problem.

Worksheet C prepares students to multiply two numbers times two numbers. Show them that 1 x 12 = 12 when the 1 is in the 1s place and 10 x 12 = 120 when the 1 is in the 10s place.

$$
\begin{array}{r}
12 \\
\times 11 \\
\hline
12 = (1 \times 12) \\
(10 \times 12) = \underline{120} \\
\hline
132
\end{array}
$$

Have students do one row and ask for the pattern for multiplying by 11. (Spread the two numbers apart and add the two numbers for the middle numeral.)

Worksheet D is a simple example of math art.

OPTIONAL: Flip folders can be made using instructions on page 7. Students write one group of facts on each page.

Each student should also have a math notebook. This can be purchased (a pocket folder) or made using instructions on page 7 of MPM. Students should keep page 11, Groups of 7, Base 10 Counting Charts and worksheets in the folder. Base 10 Counting Charts can be used with later groups of facts and worksheets can be used as study sheets.

Name _____

GROUPS OF 7

RECTANGULAR ARRAY

1 x 7 = _____

2 x 7 = _____

3 x 7 = _____

4 x 7 = _____

5 x 7 = _____

6 x 7 = _____

7 x 7 = _____

8 x 7 = _____

9 x 7 = _____

10 x 7 = _____

TLC10346 Copyright © Teaching & Learning Company, Carthage, IL 62321-0010

1	2	3	4	5	6	7	8	9	10
11	12	13	14	15	16	17	18	19	20
21	22	23	24	25	26	27	28	29	30
31	32	33	34	35	36	37	38	39	40
41	42	43	44	45	46	47	48	49	50
51	52	53	54	55	56	57	58	59	60
61	62	63	64	65	66	67	68	69	70
71	72	73	74	75	76	77	78	79	80
81	82	83	84	85	86	87	88	89	90
91	92	93	94	95	96	97	98	99	100
101	102	103	104	105	106	107	108	109	110
111	112	113	114	115	116	117	118	119	120
121	122	123	124	125	126	127	128	129	130
131	132	133	134	135	136	137	138	139	140
141	142	143	144	145	146	147	148	149	150

1	2	3	4	5	6	7	8	9	10
11	12	13	14	15	16	17	18	19	20
21	22	23	24	25	26	27	28	29	30
31	32	33	34	35	36	37	38	39	40
41	42	43	44	45	46	47	48	49	50
51	52	53	54	55	56	57	58	59	60
61	62	63	64	65	66	67	68	69	70
71	72	73	74	75	76	77	78	79	80
81	82	83	84	85	86	87	88	89	90
91	92	93	94	95	96	97	98	99	100
101	102	103	104	105	106	107	108	109	110
111	112	113	114	115	116	117	118	119	120
121	122	123	124	125	126	127	128	129	130
131	132	133	134	135	136	137	138	139	140
141	142	143	144	145	146	147	148	149	150

1	2	3	4	5	6	7	8	9	10
11	12	13	14	15	16	17	18	19	20
21	22	23	24	25	26	27	28	29	30
31	32	33	34	35	36	37	38	39	40
41	42	43	44	45	46	47	48	49	50
51	52	53	54	55	56	57	58	59	60
61	62	63	64	65	66	67	68	69	70
71	72	73	74	75	76	77	78	79	80
81	82	83	84	85	86	87	88	89	90
91	92	93	94	95	96	97	98	99	100
101	102	103	104	105	106	107	108	109	110
111	112	113	114	115	116	117	118	119	120
121	122	123	124	125	126	127	128	129	130
131	132	133	134	135	136	137	138	139	140
141	142	143	144	145	146	147	148	149	150

1	2	3	4	5	6	7	8	9	10
11	12	13	14	15	16	17	18	19	20
21	22	23	24	25	26	27	28	29	30
31	32	33	34	35	36	37	38	39	40
41	42	43	44	45	46	47	48	49	50
51	52	53	54	55	56	57	58	59	60
61	62	63	64	65	66	67	68	69	70
71	72	73	74	75	76	77	78	79	80
81	82	83	84	85	86	87	88	89	90
91	92	93	94	95	96	97	98	99	100
101	102	103	104	105	106	107	108	109	110
111	112	113	114	115	116	117	118	119	120
121	122	123	124	125	126	127	128	129	130
131	132	133	134	135	136	137	138	139	140
141	142	143	144	145	146	147	148	149	150

BASE 10 COUNTING CHARTS

TLC10346 Copyright © Teaching & Learning Company, Carthage, IL 62321-0010

SUBTRACTION FACTS

4 - 4 = 0 5 - 4 = 1 6 - 4 = 2 7 - 4 = 3 8 - 4 = 4 9 - 4 = 5 10 - 4 = 6 11 - 4 = 7 12 - 4 = 8 13 - 4 = 9

9 - 9 = 0 10 - 9 = 1 11 - 9 = 2 12 - 9 = 3 13 - 9 = 4 14 - 9 = 5 15 - 9 = 6 16 - 9 = 7 17 - 9 = 8 18 - 9 = 9

3 - 3 = 0 4 - 3 = 1 5 - 3 = 2 6 - 3 = 3 7 - 3 = 4 8 - 3 = 5 9 - 3 = 6 10 - 3 = 7 11 - 3 = 8 12 - 3 = 9

8 - 8 = 0 9 - 8 = 1 10 - 8 = 2 11 - 8 = 3 12 - 8 = 4 13 - 8 = 5 14 - 8 = 6 15 - 8 = 7 16 - 8 = 8 17 - 8 = 9

2 - 2 = 0 3 - 2 = 1 4 - 2 = 2 5 - 2 = 3 6 - 2 = 4 7 - 2 = 5 8 - 2 = 6 9 - 2 = 7 10 - 2 = 8 11 - 2 = 9

7 - 7 = 0 8 - 7 = 1 9 - 7 = 2 10 - 7 = 3 11 - 7 = 4 12 - 7 = 5 13 - 7 = 6 14 - 7 = 7 15 - 7 = 8 16 - 7 = 9

1 - 1 = 0 2 - 1 = 1 3 - 1 = 2 4 - 1 = 3 5 - 1 = 4 6 - 1 = 5 7 - 1 = 6 8 - 1 = 7 9 - 1 = 8 10 - 1 = 9

6 - 6 = 0 7 - 6 = 1 8 - 6 = 2 9 - 6 = 3 10 - 6 = 4 11 - 6 = 5 12 - 6 = 6 13 - 6 = 7 14 - 6 = 8 15 - 6 = 9

0 - 0 = 0 1 - 0 = 1 2 - 0 = 2 3 - 0 = 3 4 - 0 = 4 5 - 0 = 5 6 - 0 = 6 7 - 0 = 7 8 - 0 = 8 9 - 0 = 9

5 - 5 = 0 6 - 5 = 1 7 - 5 = 2 8 - 5 = 3 9 - 5 = 4 10 - 5 = 5 11 - 5 = 6 12 - 5 = 7 13 - 5 = 8 14 - 5 = 9

ADDITION FACTS

4 + 0 = 4 4 + 1 = 5 4 + 2 = 6 4 + 3 = 7 4 + 4 = 8 4 + 5 = 9 4 + 6 = 10 4 + 7 = 11 4 + 8 = 12 4 + 9 = 13

9 + 0 = 9 9 + 1 = 10 9 + 2 = 11 9 + 3 = 12 9 + 4 = 13 9 + 5 = 14 9 + 6 = 15 9 + 7 = 16 9 + 8 = 17 9 + 9 = 18

3 + 0 = 3 3 + 1 = 4 3 + 2 = 5 3 + 3 = 6 3 + 4 = 7 3 + 5 = 8 3 + 6 = 9 3 + 7 = 10 3 + 8 = 11 3 + 9 = 12

8 + 0 = 8 8 + 1 = 9 8 + 2 = 10 8 + 3 = 11 8 + 4 = 12 8 + 5 = 13 8 + 6 = 14 8 + 7 = 15 8 + 8 = 16 8 + 9 = 17

2 + 0 = 2 2 + 1 = 3 2 + 2 = 4 2 + 3 = 5 2 + 4 = 6 2 + 5 = 7 2 + 6 = 8 2 + 7 = 9 2 + 8 = 10 2 + 9 = 11

7 + 0 = 7 7 + 1 = 8 7 + 2 = 9 7 + 3 = 10 7 + 4 = 11 7 + 5 = 12 7 + 6 = 13 7 + 7 = 14 7 + 8 = 15 7 + 9 = 16

1 + 0 = 1 1 + 1 = 2 1 + 2 = 3 1 + 3 = 4 1 + 4 = 5 1 + 5 = 6 1 + 6 = 7 1 + 7 = 8 1 + 8 = 9 1 + 9 = 10

6 + 0 = 6 6 + 1 = 7 6 + 2 = 8 6 + 3 = 9 6 + 4 = 10 6 + 5 = 11 6 + 6 = 12 6 + 7 = 13 6 + 8 = 14 6 + 9 = 15

0 + 0 = 0 0 + 1 = 1 0 + 2 = 2 0 + 3 = 3 0 + 4 = 4 0 + 5 = 5 0 + 6 = 6 0 + 7 = 7 0 + 8 = 8 0 + 9 = 9

5 + 0 = 5 5 + 1 = 6 5 + 2 = 7 5 + 3 = 8 5 + 4 = 9 5 + 5 = 10 5 + 6 = 11 5 + 7 = 12 5 + 8 = 13 5 + 9 = 14

DIVISION FACTS

0 ÷ 5 = 0 5 ÷ 5 = 1 10 ÷ 5 = 2 15 ÷ 5 = 3 20 ÷ 5 = 4 25 ÷ 5 = 5 30 ÷ 5 = 6 35 ÷ 5 = 7 40 ÷ 5 = 8 45 ÷ 5 = 9 50 ÷ 5 = 10

0 ÷ 10 = 0 10 ÷ 10 = 1 20 ÷ 10 = 2 30 ÷ 10 = 3 40 ÷ 10 = 4 50 ÷ 10 = 5 60 ÷ 10 = 6 70 ÷ 10 = 7 80 ÷ 10 = 8 90 ÷ 10 = 9 100 ÷ 10 = 10

0 ÷ 4 = 0 4 ÷ 4 = 1 8 ÷ 4 = 2 12 ÷ 4 = 3 16 ÷ 4 = 4 20 ÷ 4 = 5 24 ÷ 4 = 6 28 ÷ 4 = 7 32 ÷ 4 = 8 36 ÷ 4 = 9 40 ÷ 4 = 10

0 ÷ 9 = 0 9 ÷ 9 = 1 18 ÷ 9 = 2 27 ÷ 9 = 3 36 ÷ 9 = 4 45 ÷ 9 = 5 54 ÷ 9 = 6 63 ÷ 9 = 7 72 ÷ 9 = 8 81 ÷ 9 = 9 90 ÷ 9 = 10

0 ÷ 3 = 0 3 ÷ 3 = 1 6 ÷ 3 = 2 9 ÷ 3 = 3 12 ÷ 3 = 4 15 ÷ 3 = 5 18 ÷ 3 = 6 21 ÷ 3 = 7 24 ÷ 3 = 8 27 ÷ 3 = 9 30 ÷ 3 = 10

0 ÷ 8 = 0 8 ÷ 8 = 1 16 ÷ 8 = 2 24 ÷ 8 = 3 32 ÷ 8 = 4 40 ÷ 8 = 5 48 ÷ 8 = 6 56 ÷ 8 = 7 64 ÷ 8 = 8 72 ÷ 8 = 9 80 ÷ 8 = 10

0 ÷ 2 = 0 2 ÷ 2 = 1 4 ÷ 2 = 2 6 ÷ 2 = 3 8 ÷ 2 = 4 10 ÷ 2 = 5 12 ÷ 2 = 6 14 ÷ 2 = 7 16 ÷ 2 = 8 18 ÷ 2 = 9 20 ÷ 2 = 10

0 ÷ 7 = 0 7 ÷ 7 = 1 14 ÷ 7 = 2 21 ÷ 7 = 3 28 ÷ 7 = 4 35 ÷ 7 = 5 42 ÷ 7 = 6 49 ÷ 7 = 7 56 ÷ 7 = 8 63 ÷ 7 = 9 70 ÷ 7 = 10

0 ÷ 1 = 0 1 ÷ 1 = 1 2 ÷ 1 = 2 3 ÷ 1 = 3 4 ÷ 1 = 4 5 ÷ 1 = 5 6 ÷ 1 = 6 7 ÷ 1 = 7 8 ÷ 1 = 8 9 ÷ 1 = 9 10 ÷ 1 = 10

0 ÷ 6 = 0 6 ÷ 6 = 1 12 ÷ 6 = 2 18 ÷ 6 = 3 24 ÷ 6 = 4 30 ÷ 6 = 5 36 ÷ 6 = 6 42 ÷ 6 = 7 48 ÷ 6 = 8 54 ÷ 6 = 9 60 ÷ 6 = 10

MULTIPLICATION FACTS

0 x 5 = 0 1 x 5 = 5 2 x 5 = 10 3 x 5 = 15 4 x 5 = 20 5 x 5 = 25 6 x 5 = 30 7 x 5 = 35 8 x 5 = 40 9 x 5 = 45 10 x 5 = 50

0 x 10 = 0 1 x 10 = 10 2 x 10 = 20 3 x 10 = 30 4 x 10 = 40 5 x 10 = 50 6 x 10 = 60 7 x 10 = 70 8 x 10 = 80 9 x 10 = 90 10 x 10 = 100

0 x 4 = 0 1 x 4 = 4 2 x 4 = 8 3 x 4 = 12 4 x 4 = 16 5 x 4 = 20 6 x 4 = 24 7 x 4 = 28 8 x 4 = 32 9 x 4 = 36 10 x 4 = 40

0 x 9 = 0 1 x 9 = 9 2 x 9 = 18 3 x 9 = 27 4 x 9 = 36 5 x 9 = 45 6 x 9 = 54 7 x 9 = 63 8 x 9 = 72 9 x 9 = 81 10 x 9 = 90

0 x 3 = 0 1 x 3 = 3 2 x 3 = 6 3 x 3 = 9 4 x 3 = 12 5 x 3 = 15 6 x 3 = 18 7 x 3 = 21 8 x 3 = 24 9 x 3 = 27 10 x 3 = 30

0 x 8 = 0 1 x 8 = 8 2 x 8 = 16 3 x 8 = 24 4 x 8 = 32 5 x 8 = 40 6 x 8 = 48 7 x 8 = 56 8 x 8 = 64 9 x 8 = 72 10 x 8 = 80

0 x 2 = 0 1 x 2 = 2 2 x 2 = 4 3 x 2 = 6 4 x 2 = 8 5 x 2 = 10 6 x 2 = 12 7 x 2 = 14 8 x 2 = 16 9 x 2 = 18 10 x 2 = 20

0 x 7 = 0 1 x 7 = 7 2 x 7 = 14 3 x 7 = 21 4 x 7 = 28 5 x 7 = 35 6 x 7 = 42 7 x 7 = 49 8 x 7 = 56 9 x 7 = 63 10 x 7 = 70

0 x 1 = 0 1 x 1 = 1 2 x 1 = 2 3 x 1 = 3 4 x 1 = 4 5 x 1 = 5 6 x 1 = 6 7 x 1 = 7 8 x 1 = 8 9 x 1 = 9 10 x 1 = 10

0 x 6 = 0 1 x 6 = 6 2 x 6 = 12 3 x 6 = 18 4 x 6 = 24 5 x 6 = 30 6 x 6 = 36 7 x 6 = 42 8 x 6 = 48 9 x 6 = 54 10 x 6 = 60

Name _____

1s, 2s & 10s

1.
2	10	1	10	1	10
x2	x6	x2	x5	x8	x8

2.
2	2	10	1	10	1
x7	x3	x7	x3	x3	x9

3.
10	1	2	2	1	2
x8	x4	x8	x4	x1	x9

4.
10	2	10	2	1	1
x7	x9	x10	x5	x10	x6

5.
1	10	10	10	2	1
x5	x9	x2	x4	x6	x7

6. You went to the bank to get cash for vacation! You handed the teller the check and got 8 ten-dollar bills in return. How much money is that? _____

7. You then had to stop and pick up packs of stamps with 9 stamps in each pack. How many stamps are in 2 packs? _____

CHALLENGE:

The bus back to your house has 3 numeral route numbers.

_____ _____ _____
100s   10s   1s

The numeral in the 100s place is twice as large as the one in the ones place. The 10s place numeral is a 5. In the 1s place is a two. What is the route number? _____

TLC10346 Copyright © Teaching & Learning Company, Carthage, IL 62321-0010

Name _____

10s & 11s

1. | 20 | 60 | 30 | 70 | 40 | 80 |
    | x2 | x2 | x2 | x2 | x2 | x2 |

2. | 50 | 90 | 200 | 600 | 300 | 700 |
    | x2 | x2 | x2 | x2 | x2 | x2 |

3. | 400 | 800 | 500 | 900 | 600 | 400 |
    | x2 | x2 | x2 | x2 | x2 | x2 |

Circle multiples of 11.

1	2	3	4	5	6	7	8	9	10
11	12	13	14	15	16	17	18	19	20
21	22	23	24	25	26	27	28	29	30
31	32	33	34	35	36	37	38	39	40
41	42	43	44	45	46	47	48	49	50
51	52	53	54	55	56	57	58	59	60
61	62	63	64	65	66	67	68	69	70
71	72	73	74	75	76	77	78	79	80
81	82	83	84	85	86	87	88	89	90
91	92	93	94	95	96	97	98	99	100

4. | 11 | 11 | 11 |
    | x4 | x9 | x3 |

5. | 11 | 11 | 11 |
    | x7 | x5 | x6 |

6. You bought 3 suitcases for $20 each. How much did you spend for the suitcases? _____

7. You brought home 2 traveller's checks worth $500 each. What was the total value of the two checks? _____

CHALLENGE:
You asked your friend how many days until vacation. She said if you took the number of days, added 3 and then multiplied the answer by 10, you would get 50. How many days are left until vacation? _____

11s & 12s

I. | 12 | 13 | 14 | 15 | 16 | 17 |
    | x11 | X11 | x11 | x11 | x11 | x11 |

2. | 23 | 24 | 25 | 26 | 27 | 28 |
    | x11 | x11 | x11 | x11 | x11 | x11 |

3. | 35 | 33 | 44 | 43 | 45 | 36 |
    | x11 | x11 | x11 | x11 | x11 | x11 |

Circle multiples of 12.

1	2	3	4	5	6	7	8	9	10
11	12	13	14	15	16	17	18	19	20
21	22	23	24	25	26	27	28	29	30
31	32	33	34	35	36	37	38	39	40
41	42	43	44	45	46	47	48	49	50
51	52	53	54	55	56	57	58	59	60
61	62	63	64	65	66	67	68	69	70
71	72	73	74	75	76	77	78	79	80
81	82	83	84	85	86	87	88	89	90
91	92	93	94	95	96	97	98	99	100

4. | 12 | 12 | 12 |
    | x3 | x4 | x5 |

5. | 12 | 12 | 12 |
    | x60 | x70 | x80 |

TLC10346 Copyright © Teaching & Learning Company, Carthage, IL 62321-0010

MATH ART

Connect the dots between pairs of problems with the same answer.

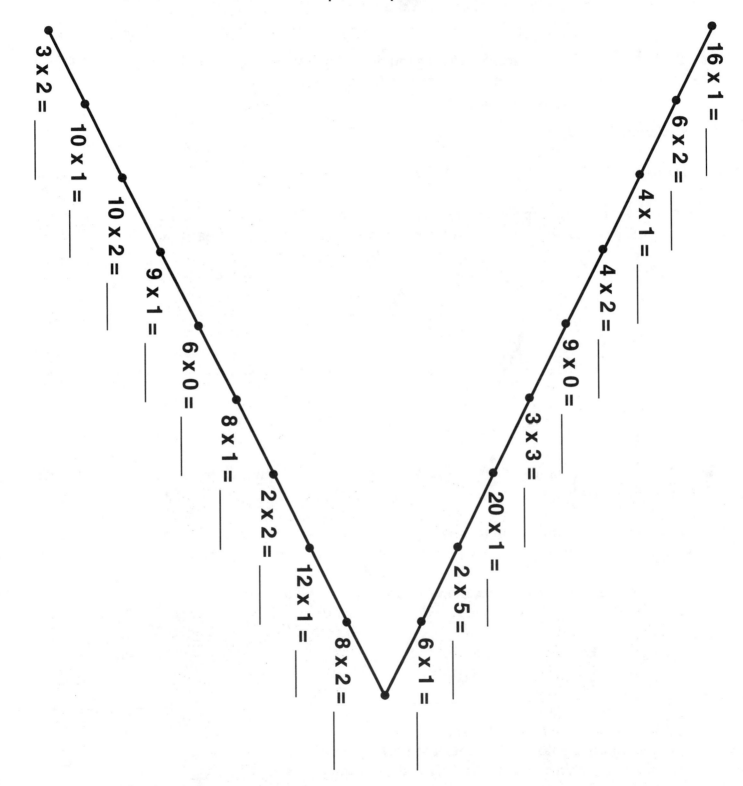

3 x 2 =

10 x 1 =

10 x 2 =

9 x 1 =

6 x 0 =

8 x 1 =

2 x 2 =

12 x 1 =

8 x 2 =

6 x 1 =

2 x 5 =

20 x 1 =

3 x 3 =

9 x 0 =

4 x 2 =

4 x 1 =

6 x 2 =

16 x 1 =

Architects and sculptors use curves such as this in their work!

TLC10346 Copyright © Teaching & Learning Company, Carthage, IL 62321-0010

LESSON PLAN 2: 5s, 9s & SQUARES

OBJECTIVE: Teach or review the groups for five and nine and also the perfect squares, where both factors (numbers being multiplied) are the same.

MATERIALS: counting charts for circling multiples 5 and 9 (page 12), T-Tables (pages 20-21), page protectors and markers (optional), worksheets (pages 22-25)

DEMONSTRATION:

5s

1. Use pages 60-62 and 70-73 in MPM as needed.

2. Pass out Worksheet E (page 22). Explain that when the minute hand goes from the 12 to the 1, 5 minutes have passed. Have students write in multiples of 5 beside each number:

Make multiplication facts:
5 x 1 = 5
5 x 2 = 10

9s

1. Use pages 22-28 in MPM as needed.

2. Have students do the top of Worksheet F (page 23). Point out that each answer has numerals which add up to 9.

3. Show them a "rainbow" for numbers pairs for 9. (See pages 15-28 in the *Math Phonics™— Addition & Subtraction Bonus Book*.) This shows which pairs of numbers equal 9.

4. For a new memory trick for 9s, see Worksheet H (page 25).

Squares

1. Use pages 15-17 in MPM as needed.
2. Give students these memory helps:
    5 x 5 ends in 5 (25)
    6 x 6 ends in 6 (36)
    7 x 7 is a football team (49ers)
    8 x 8 fell on the floor, when they got up, they were (64)
Have them write these on the back of their squares worksheet.

TLC10346 Copyright © Teaching & Learning Company, Carthage, IL 62321-0010

HANDOUT: Give each student a copy of page 20, T-Tables. This can be done in class as a practice page or used as a quiz. Tell students to keep this in their math folders to use as a study page. They can cover the answers and try to think of them.

CLASSROOM DRILL: Have students say 5s, 9s and squares facts in unison. Have students check each other to see if each one knows these facts.

WORKSHEETS: For Worksheet E, explain 22 x 5 (in the second row). Write 22 five times and add. You regroup by carrying the 1 group of 10 to the 10s column. You do the same when you multiply.

$$
\begin{array}{r}
1 \\
22 \\
22 \\
22 \\
22 \\
+22 \\
\hline
110
\end{array}
\qquad
\begin{array}{r}
22 \\
\times 5 \\
\hline
110
\end{array}
$$

For Worksheet E, 5 times an odd number ends in 5, and 5 times an even number ends in 0. For Worksheet F, 9 times an even number is an even number.

OPTIONAL: Take pictures of rectangular arrays in and around your school. (Ex: Four rows of desks with five in each row. Papers on a bulletin board—6 rows with 7 in each row.) Let teams of two students take one of the pictures and search the school for five minutes to see if they can find it.

Also, have students bring rectangular arrays from home. Checkerboards, quilts, egg cartons and muffin tins are some examples.

Name _____

T-TABLES

Top section

x0		x1		x2		x5		x9		x10		Squares	
0		0		0		0		0		0		0	
1		1		1		1		1		1		1	
2		2		2		2		2		2		2	
3		3		3		3		3		3		3	
4		4		4		4		4		4		4	
5		5		5		5		5		5		5	
6		6		6		6		6		6		6	
7		7		7		7		7		7		7	
8		8		8		8		8		8		8	
9		9		9		9		9		9		9	

Fold. Look above for help if needed.

Bottom section

x0		x1		x2		x5		x9		x10		Squares	
9		8		7		3		0		9		4	
6		5		1		0		9		6		6	
0		2		4		9		1		0		1	
3		0		0		6		8		3		3	
1		4		8		2		2		8		9	
4		1		2		8		7		7		7	
7		7		5		5		3		4		0	
2		9		3		1		6		1		8	
5		6		9		7		4		2		2	
8		3		6		4		5		5		5	

TLC10346 Copyright © Teaching & Learning Company, Carthage, IL 62321-0010

T-TABLES

Name _____

5s

Write in the minutes around this clock.

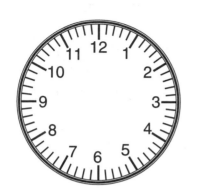

Write in the answers to the 5s.

1 x 5 = _____	2 x 5 = _____
3 x 5 = _____	4 x 5 = _____
5 x 5 = _____	6 x 5 = _____
7 x 5 = _____	8 x 5 = _____
9 x 5 = _____	10 x 5 = _____
11 x 5 = _____	12 x 5 = _____

Fold on dotted line. Look above for help.

- -

1.
1	2	3	4	5	6
x5	x5	x5	x5	x5	x5

2.
7	8	9	11	22	33
x5	x5	x5	x5	x5	x5

3.
44	55	66	77	88	99
x5	x5	x5	x5	x5	x5

4. You bought 6 T-shirts on sale for $5 each. How much was the total for the shirts? _____

5. Socks were $5 a pair. What would be the price for 9 pairs? _____

CHALLENGE:
You bought a book with puzzles to play in the car. Here's the first one: This is a magic square. Each row, column and diagonal totals 33. Fill in the missing numbers.

14		
	11	
	15	8

TLC10346 Copyright © Teaching & Learning Company, Carthage, IL 62321-0010

Name _____

9s

Circle multiples of 9.

1	2	3	4	5	6	7	8	9	10
11	12	13	14	15	16	17	18	19	20
21	22	23	24	25	26	27	28	29	30
31	32	33	34	35	36	37	38	39	40
41	42	43	44	45	46	47	48	49	50
51	52	53	54	55	56	57	58	59	60
61	62	63	64	65	66	67	68	69	70
71	72	73	74	75	76	77	78	79	80
81	82	83	84	85	86	87	88	89	90
91	92	93	94	95	96	97	98	99	100

Write in the 9s.

1 x 9 = _____   2 x 9 = _____

3 x 9 = _____   4 x 9 = _____

5 x 9 = _____   6 x 9 = _____

7 x 9 = _____   8 x 9 = _____

9 x 9 = _____   10 x 9 = _____

11 x 9 = _____

- - - - - - - - - - Fold on dotted line. Look above for help. - - - - - - - - - -

Make a rainbow of number pairs for 9.

Count by 9s.

9, 18, _____, _____, _____,

_____, _____, _____, _____, 90

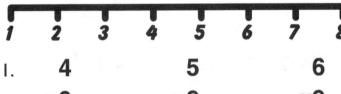

1.
4	5	6	7	8	9
x9	x9	x9	x9	x9	x9

2.
44	55	66	77	88	99
x9	x9	x9	x9	x9	x9

3. Rain ponchos sell for $9 each. How much for seven of them? _____

4. You need 9 sticks of lip balm. If they are $2 each, how much will they cost? _____

CHALLENGE:
Think of all the items beginning with a T that you could use on vacation. Write them on the back of this page. You are being hired by a travel company to use these words in a booklet they are printing. They will pay you $9 for each word. How much money will you earn? _____

TLC10346 Copyright © Teaching & Learning Company, Carthage, IL 62321-0010

Name _____

SQUARES

1 x 1 = _____   2 x 2 = _____   3 x 3 = _____

4 x 4 = _____   5 x 5 = _____   6 x 6 = _____

7 x 7 = _____   8 x 8 = _____   9 x 9 = _____

- - - - - - - - - - Fold on dotted line. Look above for help. - - - - - - - - - -

1. 4   5   6   7   8   9
    x4   x5   x6   x7   x8   x9

2. 55   99   77   66   44   88
    x9   x9   x9   x9   x9   x9

3. 9 x 90 = _____   60 x 6 = _____   40 x 4 = _____   80 x 8 = _____

4. 9 x 900 = _____   500 x 5 = _____   70 x 7 = _____   400 x 4 = _____

5. 99   99   99   99   99   99
    x1   x2   x3   x4   x5   x6

6. 44   55   66   77   88   99
    x4   x5   x6   x7   x8   x9

TLC10346 Copyright © Teaching & Learning Company, Carthage, IL 62321-0010

9s, SQUARES & 5s
(NO 0s, 1s OR 2s)

1.
$$\begin{array}{c} 9 \\ \times 4 \end{array}$$
$$\begin{array}{c} 5 \\ \times 4 \end{array}$$
$$\begin{array}{c} 7 \\ \times 7 \end{array}$$
$$\begin{array}{c} 8 \\ \times 8 \end{array}$$
$$\begin{array}{c} 9 \\ \times 6 \end{array}$$
$$\begin{array}{c} 9 \\ \times 7 \end{array}$$

2.
$$\begin{array}{c} 5 \\ \times 9 \end{array}$$
$$\begin{array}{c} 9 \\ \times 8 \end{array}$$
$$\begin{array}{c} 6 \\ \times 6 \end{array}$$
$$\begin{array}{c} 5 \\ \times 8 \end{array}$$
$$\begin{array}{c} 9 \\ \times 3 \end{array}$$
$$\begin{array}{c} 5 \\ \times 7 \end{array}$$

3.
$$\begin{array}{c} 3 \\ \times 3 \end{array}$$
$$\begin{array}{c} 5 \\ \times 6 \end{array}$$
$$\begin{array}{c} 5 \\ \times 5 \end{array}$$
$$\begin{array}{c} 9 \\ \times 9 \end{array}$$
$$\begin{array}{c} 4 \\ \times 4 \end{array}$$
$$\begin{array}{c} 5 \\ \times 3 \end{array}$$

4.
$$\begin{array}{c} 44 \\ \times 9 \end{array}$$
$$\begin{array}{c} 77 \\ \times 9 \end{array}$$
$$\begin{array}{c} 99 \\ \times 9 \end{array}$$
$$\begin{array}{c} 44 \\ \times 4 \end{array}$$
$$\begin{array}{c} 88 \\ \times 8 \end{array}$$
$$\begin{array}{c} 55 \\ \times 5 \end{array}$$

5.
$$\begin{array}{c} 66 \\ \times 5 \end{array}$$
$$\begin{array}{c} 77 \\ \times 5 \end{array}$$
$$\begin{array}{c} 33 \\ \times 5 \end{array}$$
$$\begin{array}{c} 90 \\ \times 9 \end{array}$$
$$\begin{array}{c} 400 \\ \times 4 \end{array}$$
$$\begin{array}{c} 80 \\ \times 8 \end{array}$$

Remember this 9s trick:

10 x 6 = _____	10 x 7 = _____	10 x 8 = _____	10 x 9 = _____
− 6	− 7	− 8	− 9
9 x 6 = _____	9 x 7 = _____	9 x 8 = _____	9 x 9 = _____

LESSON PLAN 3: 3s & 4s

OBJECTIVE: Teach or review 3s and 4s multiplication facts.

MATERIALS: math skills of the week poster (page 28), passes and coupons (page 29), game (page 30), flash cards for fours (pages 31-34), mini facts charts (pages 35-36), worksheets (pages 38-42)

DEMONSTRATION:

3s

1. Use Lesson Plan 8 in MPM as needed.

2. Post a Math Skill of the Week poster in the classroom. List the multiples of 3 while studying 3s. See page 65 in the *Math Phonics™—Addition & Subtraction Bonus Book* for more ideas on using the poster.
3. Teach the class Multiplication Matchup. See page 30 for directions.
4. Run off the Math Pack (page 66, in *Math Phonics™—Multiplication*) on tagboard. Decorate and laminate. Cut apart and punch a hole in the top of each card. String on a 30" shoestring with a large macaroni or three bugle beads between each two cards. Students can wear the necklace or keep it in their math folders to study.

4s

1. Use Lesson Plan 8 in MPM as needed.

2. Use the 4s flash cards (pages 31-34). If they can't think of 4 x 6, think of 2 x 6 and double the answer.

   Example: $2 \times 6 = 12$ $4 \times 6 = 24$
   $$\begin{array}{r} 12 \\ +12 \\ \hline 24 \end{array}$$

3. Give each student a set of 4s flash cards or enlarge and post them at the front of the room.

TLC10346 Copyright © Teaching & Learning Company, Carthage, IL 62321-0010

HANDOUT: Give each student a 4 x 6 index card or run off page 35 or page 36 on card stock and cut apart on double lines. If you use page 37, have students fill in the mini facts chart as shown on page 35.

This is a shorter form of a facts chart, having only facts 3 through 9. Students should not have to look up 0s, 1s, 2s or 10s. This chart can also be used to help in thinking of answers to division problems. This will be explained in Lesson Plan 4.

CLASSROOM DRILL: Have the class count by 3s for several days. Then have everyone count by 4s for several days. Review groups taught in Lesson Plan 1 if necessary.

3 6 9 12
15 18 21
24 27 30
33 36 39
42 45 48

4 8 12 16
20 24 28 32
36 40 44 48

WORKSHEETS: Use these four worksheets several times if necessary until students master the threes and fours. These groups are very difficult for many students.

OPTIONAL: Use the T-Tables on page 20 for more practice with the 3s and 4s. If students need help with 2s, use the blank mini facts chart and start with 2s—omit squares.

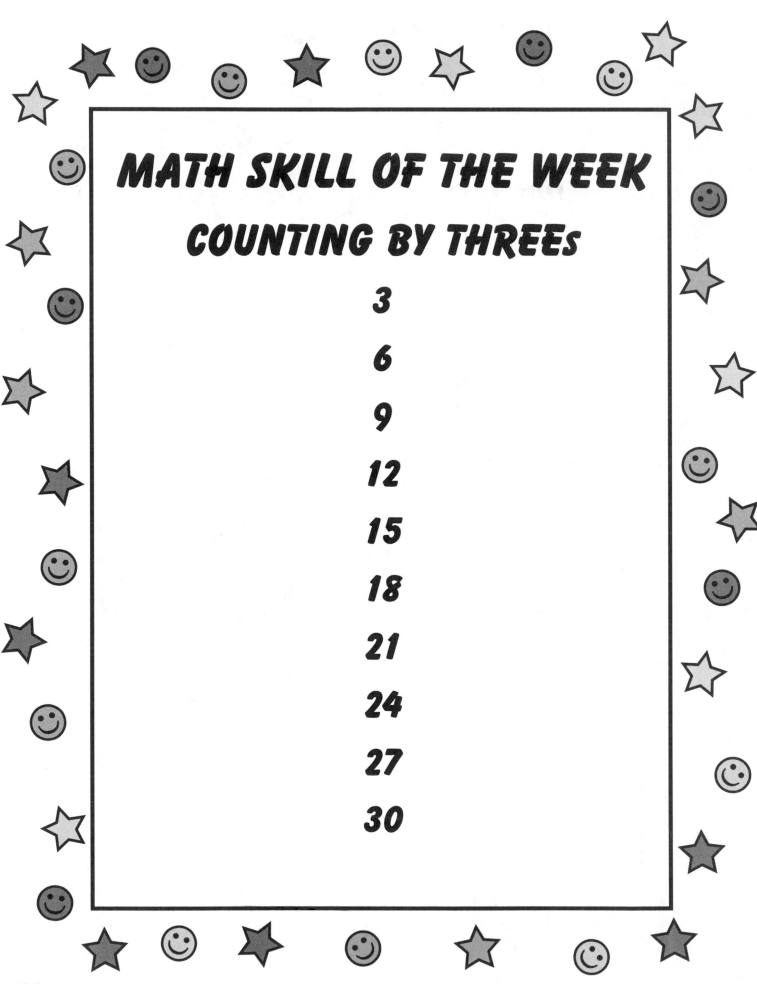

MATH SKILL OF THE WEEK

COUNTING BY THREES

3

6

9

12

15

18

21

24

27

30

TLC10346 Copyright © Teaching & Learning Company, Carthage, IL 62321-0010

HOMEWORK PASS	HOMEWORK PASS
HOMEWORK PASS	HOMEWORK PASS
PRIZE COUPON	PRIZE COUPON
PRIZE COUPON	PRIZE COUPON
PRIZE COUPON	PRIZE COUPON
PRIZE COUPON	PRIZE COUPON
PRIZE COUPON	PRIZE COUPON
PRIZE COUPON	PRIZE COUPON

MULTIPLICATION MATCHUP

MATERIALS: One index card for each student in the class.*

PREPARATION: Teacher or students can write a multiple of three on each of the index cards. Be sure there will be a variety of numbers.

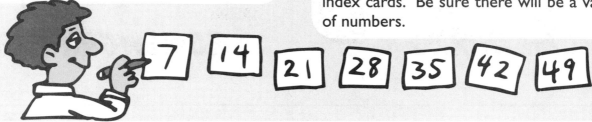

DIRECTIONS: Give each student an index card. Review the multiples of three. If students want to write their fact on another piece of paper, this is fine, but the index card should have just the answer.

Teacher or student leader calls out a fact without giving the answer—3 x 7 for example. The first student with the 21 who stands up and says 21 gets a point for his or her team. If you have a tie between two people on different teams, give both teams a point. If you have a tie between two people on the same team, give the team one point. This is more fair because there may be more than one person on a team with the same number. If a student stands who has the wrong number, subtract a point for that team.

First team to get 10 points wins. Then mix up the index cards and go again. Prizes are optional. You could ask parents to donate pencils, erasers or candy (if you could hand it out at the end of the day). After two or three rounds, you could mix up the teams and go another round or two.

*NOTE: This game will be explained as if you are teaching the multiplication facts for three. However, it can be used for any other group of facts. It could be used for addition, subtraction or division with minor changes.

TLC10346 Copyright © Teaching & Learning Company, Carthage, IL 62321-0010

$$2 \times 6 = \underline{\hspace{3cm}}$$

$$4 \times 6 = \underline{\hspace{3cm}}$$

$$2 \times 7 = \underline{\hspace{3cm}}$$

$$4 \times 7 = \underline{\hspace{3cm}}$$

TLC10346 Copyright © Teaching & Learning Company, Carthage, IL 62321-0010

$$2 \times 6 = 12$$

$$\begin{array}{r} 12 \\ +12 \\ \hline 24 \end{array}$$

$$4 \times 6 = 24$$

☺ ☺ ☺ ☺ ☺ ☺
☺ ☺ ☺ ☺ ☺ ☺
☺ ☺ ☺ ☺ ☺ ☺
☺ ☺ ☺ ☺ ☺ ☺

$$2 \times 7 = 14$$

$$\begin{array}{r} 14 \\ +14 \\ \hline 28 \end{array}$$

$$4 \times 7 = 28$$

☺ ☺ ☺ ☺ ☺ ☺ ☺
☺ ☺ ☺ ☺ ☺ ☺ ☺
☺ ☺ ☺ ☺ ☺ ☺ ☺
☺ ☺ ☺ ☺ ☺ ☺ ☺

TLC10346 Copyright © Teaching & Learning Company, Carthage, IL 62321-0010

$$2 \times 8 = \underline{\hphantom{XXXXX}}$$

$$4 \times 8 = \underline{\hphantom{XXXXX}}$$

$$2 \times 9 = \underline{\hphantom{XXXXX}}$$

$$4 \times 9 = \underline{\hphantom{XXXXX}}$$

TLC10346 Copyright © Teaching & Learning Company, Carthage, IL 62321-0010

$$2 \times 8 = 16$$

$$\begin{array}{r} 12 \\ +12 \\ \hline 24 \end{array}$$

$$4 \times 8 = 32$$

☺ ☺ ☺ ☺ ☺ ☺ ☺ ☺
☺ ☺ ☺ ☺ ☺ ☺ ☺ ☺
☺ ☺ ☺ ☺ ☺ ☺ ☺ ☺
☺ ☺ ☺ ☺ ☺ ☺ ☺ ☺

$$2 \times 9 = 18$$

$$\begin{array}{r} 14 \\ +14 \\ \hline 28 \end{array}$$

$$4 \times 9 = 36$$

☺ ☺ ☺ ☺ ☺ ☺ ☺ ☺ ☺
☺ ☺ ☺ ☺ ☺ ☺ ☺ ☺ ☺
☺ ☺ ☺ ☺ ☺ ☺ ☺ ☺ ☺
☺ ☺ ☺ ☺ ☺ ☺ ☺ ☺ ☺

TLC10346 Copyright © Teaching & Learning Company, Carthage, IL 62321-0010

6×

6 × 3 =
6 × 4 =
6 × 5 =
6 × 6 =
6 × 7 =
6 × 8 =
6 × 9 =

5×

5 × 3 =
5 × 4 =
5 × 5 =
5 × 6 =
5 × 7 =
5 × 8 =
5 × 9 =

4×

4 × 3 =
4 × 4 =
4 × 5 =
4 × 6 =
4 × 7 =
4 × 8 =
4 × 9 =

3×

3 × 3 =
3 × 4 =
3 × 5 =
3 × 6 =
3 × 7 =
3 × 8 =
3 × 9 =

Squares

3 × 3 =
4 × 4 =
5 × 5 =
6 × 6 =
7 × 7 =
8 × 8 =
9 × 9 =

9×

9 × 3 =
9 × 4 =
9 × 5 =
9 × 6 =
9 × 7 =
9 × 8 =
9 × 9 =

8×

8 × 3 =
8 × 4 =
8 × 5 =
8 × 6 =
8 × 7 =
8 × 8 =
8 × 9 =

7×

7 × 3 =
7 × 4 =
7 × 5 =
7 × 6 =
7 × 7 =
7 × 8 =
7 × 9 =

6×

6 × 3 =
6 × 4 =
6 × 5 =
6 × 6 =
6 × 7 =
6 × 8 =
6 × 9 =

5×

5 × 3 =
5 × 4 =
5 × 5 =
5 × 6 =
5 × 7 =
5 × 8 =
5 × 9 =

4×

4 × 3 =
4 × 4 =
4 × 5 =
4 × 6 =
4 × 7 =
4 × 8 =
4 × 9 =

3×

3 × 3 =
3 × 4 =
3 × 5 =
3 × 6 =
3 × 7 =
3 × 8 =
3 × 9 =

Squares

3 × 3 =
4 × 4 =
5 × 5 =
6 × 6 =
7 × 7 =
8 × 8 =
9 × 9 =

9×

9 × 3 =
9 × 4 =
9 × 5 =
9 × 6 =
9 × 7 =
9 × 8 =
9 × 9 =

8×

8 × 3 =
8 × 4 =
8 × 5 =
8 × 6 =
8 × 7 =
8 × 8 =
8 × 9 =

7×

7 × 3 =
7 × 4 =
7 × 5 =
7 × 6 =
7 × 7 =
7 × 8 =
7 × 9 =

6×

6 × 3 =
6 × 4 =
6 × 5 =
6 × 6 =
6 × 7 =
6 × 8 =
6 × 9 =

5×

5 × 3 =
5 × 4 =
5 × 5 =
5 × 6 =
5 × 7 =
5 × 8 =
5 × 9 =

4×

4 × 3 =
4 × 4 =
4 × 5 =
4 × 6 =
4 × 7 =
4 × 8 =
4 × 9 =

3×

3 × 3 =
3 × 4 =
3 × 5 =
3 × 6 =
3 × 7 =
3 × 8 =
3 × 9 =

Squares

3 × 3 =
4 × 4 =
5 × 5 =
6 × 6 =
7 × 7 =
8 × 8 =
9 × 9 =

9×

9 × 3 =
9 × 4 =
9 × 5 =
9 × 6 =
9 × 7 =
9 × 8 =
9 × 9 =

8×

8 × 3 =
8 × 4 =
8 × 5 =
8 × 6 =
8 × 7 =
8 × 8 =
8 × 9 =

7×

7 × 3 =
7 × 4 =
7 × 5 =
7 × 6 =
7 × 7 =
7 × 8 =
7 × 9 =

6×

6 × 3 =
6 × 4 =
6 × 5 =
6 × 6 =
6 × 7 =
6 × 8 =
6 × 9 =

5×

5 × 3 =
5 × 4 =
5 × 5 =
5 × 6 =
5 × 7 =
5 × 8 =
5 × 9 =

4×

4 × 3 =
4 × 4 =
4 × 5 =
4 × 6 =
4 × 7 =
4 × 8 =
4 × 9 =

3×

3 × 3 =
3 × 4 =
3 × 5 =
3 × 6 =
3 × 7 =
3 × 8 =
3 × 9 =

Squares

3 × 3 =
4 × 4 =
5 × 5 =
6 × 6 =
7 × 7 =
8 × 8 =
9 × 9 =

9×

9 × 3 =
9 × 4 =
9 × 5 =
9 × 6 =
9 × 7 =
9 × 8 =
9 × 9 =

8×

8 × 3 =
8 × 4 =
8 × 5 =
8 × 6 =
8 × 7 =
8 × 8 =
8 × 9 =

7×

7 × 3 =
7 × 4 =
7 × 5 =
7 × 6 =
7 × 7 =
7 × 8 =
7 × 9 =

Set (repeated 4 times on the page — 4 identical flashcards)

```
6 x 3 = 18      5 x 3 = 15      4 x 3 = 12      3 x 3 = 9
6 x 4 = 24      5 x 4 = 20      4 x 4 = 16      3 x 4 = 12
6 x 5 = 30      5 x 5 = 25      4 x 5 = 20      3 x 5 = 15
6 x 6 = 36      5 x 6 = 30      4 x 6 = 24      3 x 6 = 18
6 x 7 = 42      5 x 7 = 35      4 x 7 = 28      3 x 7 = 21
6 x 8 = 48      5 x 8 = 40      4 x 8 = 32      3 x 8 = 24
6 x 9 = 54      5 x 9 = 45      4 x 9 = 36      3 x 9 = 27

Squares         9 x 3 = 27      8 x 3 = 24      7 x 3 = 21
3 x 3 = 9       9 x 4 = 36      8 x 4 = 32      7 x 4 = 28
4 x 4 = 16      9 x 5 = 45      8 x 5 = 40      7 x 5 = 35
5 x 5 = 25      9 x 6 = 54      8 x 6 = 48      7 x 6 = 42
6 x 6 = 36      9 x 7 = 63      8 x 7 = 56      7 x 7 = 49
7 x 7 = 49      9 x 8 = 72      8 x 8 = 64      7 x 8 = 56
8 x 8 = 64      9 x 9 = 81      8 x 9 = 72      7 x 9 = 63
9 x 9 = 81
```

TLC10346 Copyright © Teaching & Learning Company, Carthage, IL 62321-0010

3s

Circle multiples of 3.

1	2	3	4	5	6	7	8	9	10
11	12	13	14	15	16	17	18	19	20
21	22	23	24	25	26	27	28	29	30
31	32	33	34	35	36	37	38	39	40
41	42	43	44	45	46	47	48	49	50
51	52	53	54	55	56	57	58	59	60
61	62	63	64	65	66	67	68	69	70
71	72	73	74	75	76	77	78	79	80
81	82	83	84	85	86	87	88	89	90
91	92	93	94	95	96	97	98	99	100

Write in the 3s.

$3 \times 1 =$ _____ $3 \times 7 =$ _____

$3 \times 2 =$ _____ $3 \times 8 =$ _____

$3 \times 3 =$ _____ $3 \times 9 =$ _____

$3 \times 4 =$ _____ $3 \times 10 =$ _____

$3 \times 5 =$ _____ $3 \times 11 =$ _____

$3 \times 6 =$ _____ $3 \times 12 =$ _____

Fold on dotted line. Look above for help.

1.

1	2	3	4	5	6
x3	x3	x3	x3	x3	x3

2.

7	8	9	11	44	55
x3	x3	x3	x3	x3	x3

3.

22	99	66	77	33	88
x3	x3	x3	x3	x3	x3

4.

33	33	33	33	33	33
x3	x7	x2	x8	x4	x6

5. You have packed boxes of fruit snacks with 6 packs in a box. How many packs are in 3 boxes?
_____

6. Peanuts come 3 sacks in each box. How many sacks are in 8 boxes? _____

CHALLENGE:

I'm thinking of a number. If you double my number and multiply by 3, the answer is 24. What is my number? _____

TLC10346 Copyright © Teaching & Learning Company, Carthage, IL 62321-0010

Name _____

4s

Count by 4s.

4, 8, _____, _____, _____, _____, _____, _____, _____, 40

Remember this 4s trick:

6	6		7	7		8	8		9	9
x2	x4		x2	x4		x2	x4		x2	x4
12										
+12										
24										

Fold on dotted line. Look above for help.
- -

1.
1	2	3	4	5	6
x4	x4	x4	x4	x4	x4

2.
7	8	9	11	44	55
x4	x4	x4	x4	x4	x4

3.
22	99	66	77	33	88
x4	x4	x4	x4	x4	x4

4.
44	44	44	44	44	44
x3	x5	x6	x7	x8	x9

5. Medicine for car sickness comes with 4 tablets in a pack. How many tablets in 7 packs? _____

6. You should always pack aspirin. There are 30 in a bottle. You bought 4 bottles. How many aspirin are in the 4 bottles? _____

CHALLENGE:
How many three-numeral numbers can you make from a 4, a 5 and a 6? Use each numeral only once in each number. Write the numbers on the back.

TLC10346 Copyright © Teaching & Learning Company, Carthage, IL 62321-0010

Name _____

3s & 4s

1. | 4 | 4 | 3 | 3 | 4 | 3 |
    | x2 | x8 | x1 | x9 | x4 | x7 |

2. | 4 | 4 | 3 | 4 | 3 | 4 |
    | x7 | x3 | x8 | x5 | x3 | x9 |

3. | 3 | 4 | 3 | 4 | 4 | 3 |
    | x5 | x9 | x2 | x1 | x6 | x6 |

4. | 14 | 13 | 24 | 23 | 24 | 23 |
    | x6 | x9 | x6 | x3 | x8 | x8 |

5. | 33 | 34 | 34 | 33 | 44 | 33 |
    | x4 | x7 | x3 | x4 | x2 | x5 |

CHALLENGE:

You find it on the weekend, you find it in the summer. But if you found it all the time, you really would be dumber. What is it?

B = 4   C = 5   D = 3   F = 9

| 4 x B = ____ | D x F = ____ | 3 x C = ____ | B x F = ____ | 2 x D = ____ | 2 x F = ____ | B x C = ____ |
| O | N | T | V | C | I | A |

____ ____ ____ ____ ____ ____ ____ ____
36   20   6   20   15   18   16   27

TLC10346 Copyright © Teaching & Learning Company, Carthage, IL 62321-0010

Name _____

CUMULATIVES REVIEW

1.
  1   3   5   2   9   9   8
 x3   x6   x3   x3   x3   x9   x3

2.
  4   1   10   10   2   1   5
 x8   x1   x3   x10   x4   x2   x4

3.
  2   2   1   5   3   9   3
 x2   x5   x4   x6   x4   x4   x3

4.
  2   5   3   9   4   1   6
 x6   x7   x7   x6   x4   x5   x4

5.
  5   0   1   2   4   5   9
 x5   x7   x6   x7   x7   x9   x7

6.
  5   6   0   10   10   2   1
 x8   x6   x8   x4   x6   x8   x7

7.
 10   0   10   7   1   9   2
 x1   x9   x5   x7   x8   x8   x9

8.
 10   1   8   10   10   10   10
 x7   x9   x8   x2   x0   x8   x9

TLC10346 Copyright © Teaching & Learning Company, Carthage, IL 62321-0010

Name _____

MATH ART

Connect the dots between problems with the same answer.

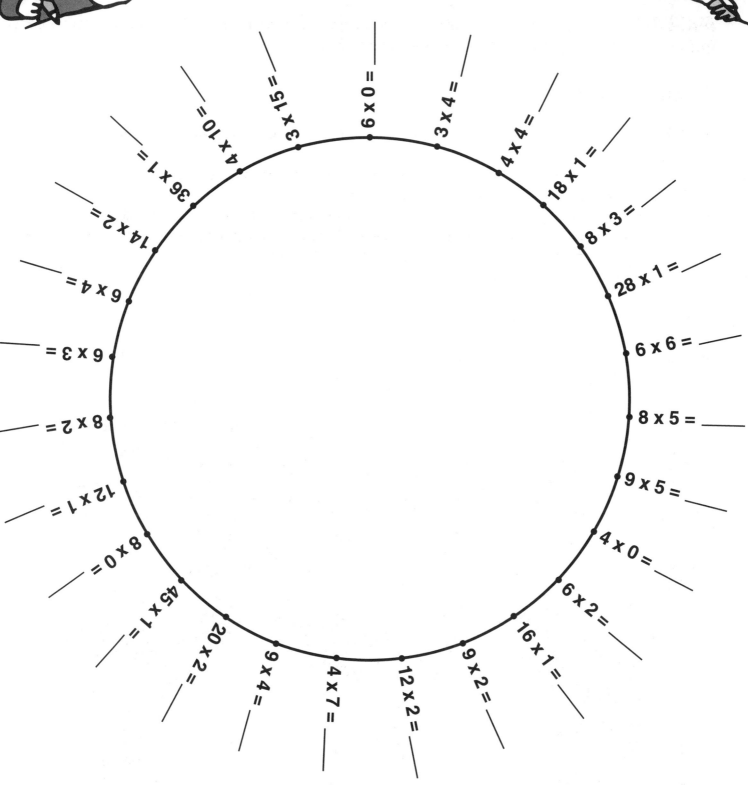

$4 \times 10 =$ ___
$3 \times 15 =$ ___
$6 \times 9 =$ ___
$3 \times 4 =$ ___
$4 \times 4 =$ ___
$36 \times 1 =$ ___
$18 \times 1 =$ ___
$14 \times 2 =$ ___
$8 \times 3 =$ ___
$6 \times 4 =$ ___
$28 \times 1 =$ ___
$6 \times 3 =$ ___
$6 \times 6 =$ ___
$8 \times 2 =$ ___
$8 \times 5 =$ ___
$12 \times 1 =$ ___
$9 \times 5 =$ ___
$8 \times 0 =$ ___
$4 \times 0 =$ ___
$45 \times 1 =$ ___
$6 \times 2 =$ ___
$20 \times 2 =$ ___
$16 \times 1 =$ ___
$9 \times 4 =$ ___
$9 \times 2 =$ ___
$4 \times 7 =$ ___
$12 \times 2 =$ ___

This math art looks like the amusement park ferris wheel.

42

TLC10346 Copyright © Teaching & Learning Company, Carthage, IL 62321-0010

LESSON PLAN 4: 6s, 7s & 8s

OBJECTIVE: Review the multiplication facts for 6s, 7s and 8s.

MATERIALS: rectangular arrays, blank multiplication facts chart (page 47), practice facts page (page 49), Math Tactics game (page 48), worksheets (pages 49-53)

DEMONSTRATION:

6s

1. Give each student page 45, Groups of 6. Have them complete the page and practice counting by 6.
2. Recall the trick to remember 6 x 4 (page 26) and the flash cards (pages 31-32).
3. For the Math Skill of the Week poster, use multiples of six.
4. For Worksheet R (page 53), review multiplying when zeros are involved. (See page 78 in *Math Phonics™—Fractions & Decimals Bonus Book* under Worksheets.) (Multiplying the non-zero numbers. Count the zeros in the problem. Put that many zeros in the answer.)

7s

Repeat the steps given for 6s. Use page 11, Groups of 7.

8s

Repeat the steps given for 6s. Use page 46, Groups of 8.

HANDOUT: Blank T-Tables, page 21. Teacher fills in a T-Table for threes, fours, sixes, sevens and eights—top in order, lower tables, not in order. Students fill in answers. Use as practice page, quiz or both. Add earlier groups, if desired.

CLASSROOM DRILL: Have the class chant multiples of six until all have mastered them. Then chant the 6s facts in order. Do the same for 7s and 8s.

WORKSHEETS: Multiplying two numbers by one with carrying. Review explanation on page 19 if necessary.

For problems like the last row on Worksheet J (page 39), students need to be able to add correctly. Review if necessary. Use the mini facts chart, page 25 in *Math Phonics™–Addition & Subtraction Bonus Book*. Also, page 13 in this book contains all basic facts for addition, subtraction, multiplication and division.

OPTIONAL: Blank multiplication facts chart—numbers are in order at the left and at the top—use as a study sheet. Then, later, use as a quiz. Also, roll two dice (ex: 3 & 4). Fill in 3 x 3, 4 x 4 and 3 x 4. Use square tissue boxes as giant dice. On one die, change four sides to 7, 8, 9 and 10 using stickers.

PRACTICE FACTS PAGE: This can also be used for students to drill these facts.

MATH TACTICS CLASSROOM TOURNAMENT: Use page 48, the scorecard for Math Tactics. Follow directions. For each turn, students may roll three times. After first roll, keep the dice which are best and roll the others again. Do the same with the second roll.

Example:
First roll: Dice are 3, 4, 6, 6, 7. Keep the two 6s and roll again.
Second roll: Dice are 6, 6, 6, 7, 8. Keep the three 6s and roll again.
Third roll: Dice are 6, 6, 6, 4, 4. Use the 6s for the score. (18 points in the third row.)

TLC10346 Copyright © Teaching & Learning Company, Carthage, IL 62321-0010

GROUPS OF 6

1 x 6 = _____

2 x 6 = _____

3 x 6 = _____

4 x 6 = _____

5 x 6 = _____

6 x 6 = _____

7 x 6 = _____

8 x 6 = _____

9 x 6 = _____

10 x 6 = _____

TLC10346 Copyright © Teaching & Learning Company, Carthage, IL 62321-0010

GROUPS OF 8

1 x 8 = _____

2 x 8 = _____

3 x 8 = _____

4 x 8 = _____

5 x 8 = _____

6 x 8 = _____

7 x 8 = _____

8 x 8 = _____

9 x 8 = _____

10 x 8 = _____

TLC10346 Copyright © Teaching & Learning Company, Carthage, IL 62321-0010

MULTIPLICATION FACTS CHART

	1	2	3	4	5	6	7	8	9	10
1										
2										
3										
4										
5										
6										
7										
8										
9										
10										

TLC10346 Copyright © Teaching & Learning Company, Carthage, IL 62321-0010

MATH TACTICS
SCORECARD

Name _____

Upper Section

4s	Count & add 4s					
5s	Count & add 5s					
6s	Count & add 6s					
7s	Count & add 7s					
8s	Count & add 8s					
9s	Count & add 9s					
TOTAL	⟶					
BONUS (If total is over 65)	Add 35					
TOTAL	⟶					

Lower Section

3 OF A KIND	Add all dice					
2 PAIRS	Add all dice					
LARGEST PRODUCT OF 2 DICE	Product only					
IF PRODUCT IS 49 OR MORE	Add 25 points					
TACTICS–4 IN A ROW	Add 50 points					
HIT OR MISS	Add all dice					
LOWER TOTAL	⟶					
UPPER TOTAL	⟶					
GRAND TOTAL	⟶					

DIRECTIONS:

Use five dice. On each die cover 1, 2 and 3 with small stickers. Write 7 over the 1, 8 over each 2 and 9 over each 3. Players complete upper section by taking turns six times. You must take a score each time—even if it is zero. Total upper scores—then complete lower section with five turns each. Fill blanks in any order.

TLC10346 Copyright © Teaching & Learning Company, Carthage, IL 62321-0010

PRACTICE FACTS PAGE

Fill in the top, fold, then fill in lower part. Refer to top if necessary.

3 x 3 = _____   3 x 4 = _____   3 x 5 = _____

4 x 3 = _____   4 x 4 = _____   4 x 5 = _____

5 x 3 = _____   5 x 4 = _____   5 x 5 = _____

6 x 3 = _____   6 x 4 = _____   6 x 5 = _____

7 x 3 = _____   7 x 4 = _____   7 x 5 = _____

8 x 3 = _____   8 x 4 = _____   8 x 5 = _____

9 x 3 = _____   9 x 4 = _____   9 x 5 = _____

3 x 6 = _____   3 x 7 = _____   3 x 8 = _____   3 x 9 = _____

4 x 6 = _____   4 x 7 = _____   4 x 8 = _____   4 x 9 = _____

5 x 6 = _____   5 x 7 = _____   5 x 8 = _____   5 x 9 = _____

6 x 6 = _____   6 x 7 = _____   6 x 8 = _____   6 x 9 = _____

7 x 6 = _____   7 x 7 = _____   7 x 8 = _____   7 x 9 = _____

8 x 6 = _____   8 x 7 = _____   8 x 8 = _____   8 x 9 = _____

9 x 6 = _____   9 x 7 = _____   9 x 8 = _____   9 x 9 = _____

1.	3 x6	4 x8	6 x7	3 x7	4 x7	6 x8	7 x8
2.	3 x8	6 x5	7 x7	9 x8	7 x9	8 x5	7 x5
3.	6 x9	9 x4	9 x3	5 x5	9 x9	9 x5	6 x4
4.	8 x8	9 x5	3 x5	4 x5	3 x4	6 x6	7 x8

TLC10346 Copyright © Teaching & Learning Company, Carthage, IL 62321-0010

6s

Circle multiples of 6.

1	2	3	4	5	6	7	8	9	10
11	12	13	14	15	16	17	18	19	20
21	22	23	24	25	26	27	28	29	30
31	32	33	34	35	36	37	38	39	40
41	42	43	44	45	46	47	48	49	50
51	52	53	54	55	56	57	58	59	60
61	62	63	64	65	66	67	68	69	70
71	72	73	74	75	76	77	78	79	80
81	82	83	84	85	86	87	88	89	90
91	92	93	94	95	96	97	98	99	100

Write in the 6s.

$6 \times 1 = $ _____ $6 \times 7 = $ _____

$6 \times 2 = $ _____ $6 \times 8 = $ _____

$6 \times 3 = $ _____ $6 \times 9 = $ _____

$6 \times 4 = $ _____ $6 \times 10 = $ _____

$6 \times 5 = $ _____ $6 \times 11 = $ _____

$6 \times 6 = $ _____ $6 \times 12 = $ _____

- - - - - - - - - - - - - - - Fold on dotted line. Look above for help. - - - - - - - - - - - - - - -

1.
$$\begin{array}{r} 6 \\ \times 1 \\ \hline \end{array} \quad \begin{array}{r} 6 \\ \times 2 \\ \hline \end{array} \quad \begin{array}{r} 6 \\ \times 3 \\ \hline \end{array} \quad \begin{array}{r} 6 \\ \times 4 \\ \hline \end{array} \quad \begin{array}{r} 6 \\ \times 5 \\ \hline \end{array} \quad \begin{array}{r} 6 \\ \times 6 \\ \hline \end{array}$$

2.
$$\begin{array}{r} 6 \\ \times 7 \\ \hline \end{array} \quad \begin{array}{r} 6 \\ \times 8 \\ \hline \end{array} \quad \begin{array}{r} 6 \\ \times 9 \\ \hline \end{array} \quad \begin{array}{r} 16 \\ \times 2 \\ \hline \end{array} \quad \begin{array}{r} 26 \\ \times 3 \\ \hline \end{array} \quad \begin{array}{r} 66 \\ \times 2 \\ \hline \end{array}$$

3.
$$\begin{array}{r} 36 \\ \times 2 \\ \hline \end{array} \quad \begin{array}{r} 26 \\ \times 4 \\ \hline \end{array} \quad \begin{array}{r} 16 \\ \times 4 \\ \hline \end{array} \quad \begin{array}{r} 46 \\ \times 2 \\ \hline \end{array} \quad \begin{array}{r} 36 \\ \times 3 \\ \hline \end{array} \quad \begin{array}{r} 26 \\ \times 5 \\ \hline \end{array}$$

4.
$$\begin{array}{r} 22 \\ \times 6 \\ \hline \end{array} \quad \begin{array}{r} 33 \\ \times 6 \\ \hline \end{array} \quad \begin{array}{r} 44 \\ \times 6 \\ \hline \end{array} \quad \begin{array}{r} 55 \\ \times 6 \\ \hline \end{array} \quad \begin{array}{r} 66 \\ \times 6 \\ \hline \end{array} \quad \begin{array}{r} 77 \\ \times 6 \\ \hline \end{array}$$

5. You and your friend bought 4 six-packs of soda. How many cans of soda did you buy?

_____

6. A giant pack of gum has 16 sticks. You bought 13 packs. How many sticks of gum is that in all?

_____

CHALLENGE:
You asked your friend how many days you will be gone on vacation. She said to think of the largest perfect square with only one numeral. That's how many days? How many days will you be gone? _____

TLC10346 Copyright © Teaching & Learning Company, Carthage, IL 62321-0010

Name _____

7s

Circle multiples of 7.

1	2	3	4	5	6	7	8	9	10
11	12	13	14	15	16	17	18	19	20
21	22	23	24	25	26	27	28	29	30
31	32	33	34	35	36	37	38	39	40
41	42	43	44	45	46	47	48	49	50
51	52	53	54	55	56	57	58	59	60
61	62	63	64	65	66	67	68	69	70
71	72	73	74	75	76	77	78	79	80
81	82	83	84	85	86	87	88	89	90
91	92	93	94	95	96	97	98	99	100

Write in the 7s.

7 x 1 = _____   7 x 6 = _____

7 x 2 = _____   7 x 7 = _____

7 x 3 = _____   7 x 8 = _____

7 x 4 = _____   7 x 9 = _____

7 x 5 = _____   7 x 10 = _____

- - - - - - - - - - - - - - - Fold on dotted line. Look above for help. - - - - - - - - - - - - - - -

1.
0	1	2	3	4	5
x7	x7	x7	x7	x7	x7

2.
6	8	9	10	11	12
x7	x7	x7	x7	x7	x7

3.
77	77	77	77	77	77
x11	x12	x13	x14	x15	x16

4. People going on the trip are: you, your mom and dad, your brother and sister and your grandma and grandpa. Your mom packed three candy bars for each person. How many candy bars did she pack? _____

5. You stopped for breakfast the first morning. Breakfast was $8 per person. How much was the total bill for breakfast? _____

CHALLENGE:
This design was on one of the highway signs. How many triangles can you find? Look for several different sizes.

8s

Circle multiples of 8.

1	2	3	4	5	6	7	8	9	10
11	12	13	14	15	16	17	18	19	20
21	22	23	24	25	26	27	28	29	30
31	32	33	34	35	36	37	38	39	40
41	42	43	44	45	46	47	48	49	50
51	52	53	54	55	56	57	58	59	60
61	62	63	64	65	66	67	68	69	70
71	72	73	74	75	76	77	78	79	80
81	82	83	84	85	86	87	88	89	90
91	92	93	94	95	96	97	98	99	100

Write in the 8s.

$8 \times 1 =$ _____ $8 \times 7 =$ _____

$8 \times 2 =$ _____ $8 \times 8 =$ _____

$8 \times 3 =$ _____ $8 \times 9 =$ _____

$8 \times 4 =$ _____ $8 \times 10 =$ _____

$8 \times 5 =$ _____ $8 \times 11 =$ _____

$8 \times 6 =$ _____ $8 \times 12 =$ _____

- - - - - - - - - - - - - Fold on dotted line. Look above for help. - - - - - - - - - - - - -

1.
1	2	3	4	5	6
x8	x8	x8	x8	x8	x8

2.
7	8	9	88	88	88
x8	x8	x8	x2	x3	x4

3.
28	38	48	58	68	78
x11	x12	x21	x32	x21	x22

4. The amusement park admission is $8 per person. What will be the total cost for the 7 people in your group? _____

5. The lines are long. You see that it takes you about 18 minutes for each ride. If there are six more rides, how long will it take for you to ride all of those rides? _____

CHALLENGE:
In this magic square, the sum is the same for each row, column and diagonal of numbers. Fill in the missing numbers.

	8	64
	40	
	72	

TLC10346 Copyright © Teaching & Learning Company, Carthage, IL 62321-0010

REVIEW—3s, 4s, 6s, 7s & 8s

1.	6 x5	3 x3	7 x5	8 x5	3 x8	4 x7
2.	8 x8	4 x4	3 x4	6 x6	7 x7	3 x9
3.	4 x8	7 x9	4 x5	3 x6	6 x7	7 x8
4.	6 x9	4 x9	8 x9	4 x6	3 x7	6 x8
5.	70 x6	90 x9	60 x8	500 x4	800 x7	500 x3
6.	26 x2	37 x3	66 x2	77 x3	88 x2	88 x3
7.	36 x12	47 x11	58 x12	62 x18	73 x21	84 x22

OBJECTIVE: Demonstrate the basic concept of division and show how it relates to multiplication.

MATERIALS: Three-Way Flash Cards (pages 57-59), mini facts charts (pages 35-36), Wall Chart A (page 56), worksheets (pages 60-64)

DEMONSTRATION:

Basic Concept of Division

1. Use this example—if 2 kids want to share 6 pieces of candy, how many will each one get? When the student gives the answer of 3, tell them they have just done their first division problem.

$$2 \text{ kids} \overline{\smash{)}\ 6 \text{ pieces candy}}^{\textstyle 3 \text{ pieces each}}$$

2. Every division problem uses the three numbers of a multiplication problem.

$$3 \times 2 = 6 \qquad\qquad 2\,\overline{\smash{)}}^{\textstyle \times\ \ 3} = 6$$

3. Use some other small numbers as examples.

TLC10346 Copyright © Teaching & Learning Company, Carthage, IL 62321-0010

HANDOUT: Give each student or pair or students a set of three-way flash cards, or have them make their own on 3" x 5" index cards cut in half.

CLASSROOM DRILL: Give students a multiplication problem: 4 x 5 =

Ask them to give the answer and the two division facts which can be made from these three numbers.

MENTAL DIVISION GAME: To make the classroom drill into a game, divide the class into two teams. Use the Three-Way Flash Cards. Read a multiplication fact. Give one point for each correct division problem that the student can give. Keep track of points on the board. Winning team can get a prize such as a pencil or a piece of gum.

For a different approach, keep everyone in one group. Tell them to give their answers as quickly as possible and see how many points they can get in five minutes. Do the same the next day. If they can beat their yesterday's time, give everyone in the class 10 bonus point on the next homework paper.

WORKSHEETS: Talk about the two numbers in a multiplication fact being called factors. Worksheets are self-explanatory.

OPTIONAL: If students need more help in understanding division, use Lesson Plan I in *Math Phonics™–Division*.

Students can use mini fact charts for multiplication to find answers to division problems. For example, if the problem is

$$7\overline{)42}$$

look at the group of facts for seven. Go down the list of answers until you see the 42. 6 x 7 = 42 Therefore,

$$\begin{array}{r} x\ 6 \\ \hline 7\overline{)}\ = 42 \end{array}$$

It may help some students to put in the times sign and equals sign. (See Wall Chart A on page 56).

ARE YOU STUMPED?

$$7\overline{)56}$$

Look at the Mini Facts Chart under the 7.

Stop when you get to 56.

$$7 \times 8 = 56 \text{ so}$$

$$7\overline{)}\begin{array}{c}\times\ 8\\=56\end{array}$$

$$56 \div 7 = 8 \text{ and}$$
$$56 \div 8 = 7$$

TLC10346 Copyright © Teaching & Learning Company, Carthage, IL 62321-0010

2 2 4	2 3 6	2 4 8
2 5 10	2 6 12	2 7 14
2 8 16	2 9 18	2 10 20
3 3 9	3 4 12	3 5 15
3 6 18	3 7 21	3 8 24
3 9 27	3 10 30	4 4 16

TLC10346 Copyright © Teaching & Learning Company, Carthage, IL 62321-0010

4 5	4 6	4 7
20	24	28
4 8	**4 9**	**4 10**
32	**36**	**40**
5 5	5 6	5 7
25	30	35
5 8	**5 9**	**5 10**
40	**45**	**50**
6 6	6 7	6 8
36	42	48
6 9	**6 10**	**7 7**
54	**60**	**49**

TLC10346 Copyright © Teaching & Learning Company, Carthage, IL 62321-0010

7	8	7	9	7	10
	56		63		70
8	8	8	9	8	10
	64		72		80
9	9	9	10	10	10
	81		90		100

DIVISION—2s & 3s

1.
| 3 | 4 | 5 | 6 | 7 | 8 | 9 |
| x2 | x2 | x2 | x2 | x2 | x2 | x2 |

2.
| 3 | 4 | 5 | 6 | 7 | 8 | 9 |
| x3 | x3 | x3 | x3 | x3 | x3 | x3 |

Fold on dotted line. Look above for help.

----

3. 4 x _____ = 8   5 x _____ = 10   _____ x 2 = 12   _____ x 2 = 14

4. 8 x _____ = 16   9 x _____ = 18   4 x _____ = 12   5 x _____ = 15

5. _____ x 6 = 18   _____ x 7 = 21   _____ x 8 = 24   _____ x 9 = 27

----

6. x $\overline{2}$

   $4\overline{)=8}$ $5\overline{)10}$ $2\overline{)12}$ $2\overline{)14}$ $8\overline{)16}$ $9\overline{)18}$

7.
   $4\overline{)12}$ $5\overline{)15}$ $3\overline{)18}$ $7\overline{)21}$ $3\overline{)24}$ $9\overline{)27}$

8. You need a few more ride tickets. They are $3 each. Your dad spent $27. How many tickets did he buy? _____

9. The souvenirs you bought for your 7 friends cost $28. How much did you spend on each person? _____

CHALLENGE:
The receipt for drinks did not print correctly. Fill in the missing numbers:

$$\begin{array}{r} \$2.40 \\ \$1.7\square \\ +\$3.\square 5 \\ \hline \$\square.43 \end{array}$$

TLC10346 Copyright © Teaching & Learning Company, Carthage, IL 62321-0010

DIVISION–4s & 5s

1. | 3 | 4 | 5 | 6 | 7 | 8 | 9 |
    | x4 | x4 | x4 | x4 | x4 | x4 | x4 |

2. | 3 | 4 | 5 | 6 | 7 | 8 | 9 |
    | x5 | x5 | x5 | x5 | x5 | x5 | x5 |

Fold on dotted line. Look above for help.
----

3. 4 x _____ = 16   4 x _____ = 20   _____ x 6 = 24   _____ x 7 = 28

4. 4 x _____ = 32   4 x _____ = 36   5 x _____ = 20   5 x _____ = 25

5. _____ x 6 = 30   _____ x 7 = 35   5 x _____ = 40   5 x _____ = 45

----

6. x ___4___
    4)=16   5)20   6)24   4)28   4)32   9)36

7.
    4)20   5)25   6)30   5)35   8)40   5)45

8. You are taking packs of stickers to your cousins with 4 in each pack. If you have 32 stickers, how many packs will that be? _____

9. Your friend knows you are collecting nickels. She hands you some nickels and says that you are holding 45 cents. How many nickels did she hand you? _____

CHALLENGE:
Why is "U" the happiest letter? Do these problems and decode the secret answer.

M 4)28	T 4)20	N 4)32	E 4)12	L 5x2=___	F 5)5
S 4)36	H 4)24	D 6)12	I 7)28	O 3x5=___	U 3x4=___

4	5	9	4	8	5	6	3

7	4	2	2	10	3	15	1

___ ___ ___!
 1 12 8

TLC10346 Copyright © Teaching & Learning Company, Carthage, IL 62321-0010

DIVISION—6s, & 7s

1.
3	4	5	6	7	8	9
x6	x6	x6	x6	x6	x6	x6

2.
3	4	5	6	7	8	9
x7	x7	x7	x7	x7	x7	x7

Fold on dotted line. Look above for help.

----

3. $6 \times \underline{\quad} = 24$ $6 \times \underline{\quad} = 30$ $\underline{\quad} \times 6 = 36$ $\underline{\quad} \times 7 = 42$

4. $\underline{\quad} \times 8 = 48$ $\underline{\quad} \times 9 = 54$ $\underline{\quad} \times 4 = 28$ $7 \times \underline{\quad} = 35$

5. $6 \times \underline{\quad} = 42$ $7 \times \underline{\quad} = 49$ $7 \times \underline{\quad} = 56$ $\underline{\quad} \times 9 = 63$

----

6. x

$3\overline{)} = 18$ $6\overline{)24}$ $6\overline{)30}$ $6\overline{)36}$ $7\overline{)42}$ $8\overline{)48}$

7.

$9\overline{)54}$ $7\overline{)35}$ $6\overline{)42}$ $7\overline{)49}$ $8\overline{)56}$ $7\overline{)63}$

8. There are 6 people in each seat of the amusement park train. If the train holds 54 people, how many seats are there? _____

9. The sign says a trainload leaves every 7 minutes. How many trainloads can leave in 42 minutes?

_____

CHALLENGE:
Connect the dots for these multiples of 7 in order. Then draw a line from the largest multiple back to the 7. Remember that the first 4 multiples of 7 are on a calendar—the 7 and the three numbers under it.

7•

42•   •28

21•   •49

56•   •14

35•

TLC10346 Copyright © Teaching & Learning Company, Carthage, IL 62321-0010

DIVISION-8s & 9s

1.
3	4	5	6	7	8	9
x8	x8	x8	x8	x8	x8	x8

2.
3	4	5	6	7	8	9
x9	x9	x9	x9	x9	x9	x9

Fold on dotted line. Look above for help.
----

3. $8 \times \underline{\quad} = 32$ $8 \times \underline{\quad} = 40$ $6 \times \underline{\quad} = 48$ $7 \times \underline{\quad} = 56$

4. $\underline{\quad} \times 8 = 64$ $8 \times \underline{\quad} = 72$ $4 \times \underline{\quad} = 36$ $5 \times \underline{\quad} = 45$

5. $\underline{\quad} \times 9 = 54$ $\underline{\quad} \times 9 = 63$ $8 \times \underline{\quad} = 72$ $9 \times \underline{\quad} = 81$

----

6. **x**

$8\overline{)=32}$ $8\overline{)40}$ $6\overline{)48}$ $7\overline{)56}$ $8\overline{)64}$ $8\overline{)72}$

7.

$4\overline{)36}$ $5\overline{)45}$ $9\overline{)54}$ $9\overline{)63}$ $8\overline{)72}$ $9\overline{)81}$

8. The "guess your weight" man says he misses one time out of eight. If he guesses the weight of 24 people, how many times does he miss? _____

9. The cost for the evening show was $63 for 7 tickets. How much was a ticket for one person? _____

CHALLENGE:

Do these problems. Make up a quick rule for problems like this. Write it on the back.

10	20	20	200
x10	x10	x30	x30

TLC10346 Copyright © Teaching & Learning Company, Carthage, IL 62321-0010

Name _____

PYRAMID AT THE PARK

The pyramid near the amusement park theater is designed to look like the pyramid at the entrance to the Louvre Museum in Paris, France. For the sentences below, if the math problem is true, draw a line between the two letters which are named. If the math problem is not true, do not draw the line. Use your mini facts chart if needed. The first one is done for you.

1. **If 9 x 5 = 45, draw a line from A to I.**
2. **If 6 x 8 = 46, draw a line from A to H.**
3. **If 7 x 7 = 49, draw a line from A to E.**
4. **If 5 x 7 = 35, draw a line from A to M.**
5. **If 6 x 4 = 25, draw a line from A to J.**
6. **If 5 x 3 = 15, draw a line from M to I.**
7. **If 8 x 8 = 64, draw a line from I to E.**
8. **If 9 x 8 = 72, draw a line from D to F.**
9. **If 3 x 8 = 22, draw a line from A to G.**
10. **If 4 x 7 = 28, draw a line from C to G.**
11. **If 42 ÷ 6 = 7, draw a line from B to H.**
12. **If 81 ÷ 9 = 9, draw a line from P to J.**
13. **If 63 ÷ 9 = 7, draw a line from O to K.**
14. **If 54 ÷ 9 = 6, draw a line from N to L.**
15. **If 45 ÷ 9 = 5, draw a line from L to Q.**
16. **If 18 ÷ 3 = 6, draw a line from K to R.**
17. **If 16 ÷ 4 = 4, draw a line from H to S.**
18. **If 12 ÷ 3 = 4, draw a line from F to Q.**
19. **If 40 ÷ 8 = 5, draw a line from J to S.**
20. **If 48 ÷ 6 = 7, draw a line from J to H.**
21. **If 56 ÷ 8 = 9, draw a line from B to P.**
22. **If 49 ÷ 7 = 7, draw a line from R to G.**
23. **If 28 ÷ 7 = 3, draw a line from K to G.**
24. **If 25 ÷ 5 = 4, draw a line from A to L.**

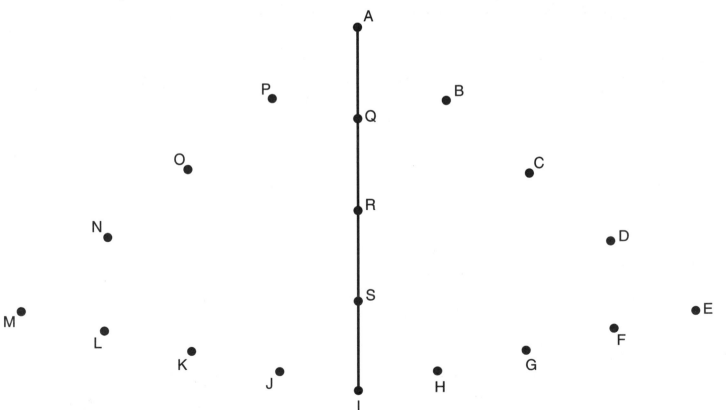

CHALLENGE:
Find a photograph of this pyramid in an encyclopedia, travel book or on the internet. Make a copy and bring it to class.

TLC10346 Copyright © Teaching & Learning Company, Carthage, IL 62321-0010

OBJECTIVE: Teach or review division for perfect squares and problems in which nine is the divisor or the quotient (answer).

MATERIALS: worksheets (pages 66-68), mini facts charts (pages 35-36) (optional)

HANDOUT: If necessary, give each student a copy of the Perfect Squares Activity sheet, page 17 in MPM or page 24 in *Math Phonics™–Division*. Follow directions given in those books.

CLASSROOM DRILL: Go around the room giving each student a multiplication problem. Student gives the answer and then gives the division problems made from the same three numbers.

WORKSHEETS: For Worksheet Y (page 67), do the first two problems in class.

$$3\overline{)9}\quad\text{with } 3 \text{ above}$$

For the second problem,

$$3\overline{)90}\quad\text{with } 30 \text{ above}$$

cover the 0 and write the 3 above the 9. We know that we must be able to make a multiplication problem with the divisor and the quotient (answer). In order to get a product of 90, we need the answer to be 30 rather than 3.

In the third problem, what number times 30 equals 90? The answer is 3 and it goes above the 0.

$$\begin{array}{c} x \qquad 3 \\ 30\overline{)} = 90 \end{array}$$

30 will not go into the 9 so you can't put the 3 above the 9. Put in the x and = signs if it helps.

OPTIONAL: Treasure Trove Island–Practice thinking of number pairs equal to nine. This is the test for divisibility by nine.

DIVISION-9s

Circle multiples of 9.

1	2	3	4	5	6	7	8	9	10
11	12	13	14	15	16	17	18	19	20
21	22	23	24	25	26	27	28	29	30
31	32	33	34	35	36	37	38	39	40
41	42	43	44	45	46	47	48	49	50
51	52	53	54	55	56	57	58	59	60
61	62	63	64	65	66	67	68	69	70
71	72	73	74	75	76	77	78	79	80
81	82	83	84	85	86	87	88	89	90
91	92	93	94	95	96	97	98	99	100

Fill in these answers.

9 x 1 = _____	9 ÷ 9 = _____	9 ÷ 1 = _____
9 x 2 = _____	18 ÷ 9 = _____	18 ÷ 2 = _____
9 x 3 = _____	27 ÷ 9 = _____	27 ÷ 3 = _____
9 x 4 = _____	36 ÷ 9 = _____	36 ÷ 4 = _____
9 x 5 = _____	45 ÷ 9 = _____	45 ÷ 5 = _____
9 x 6 = _____	54 ÷ 9 = _____	54 ÷ 6 = _____
9 x 7 = _____	63 ÷ 9 = _____	63 ÷ 7 = _____
9 x 8 = _____	72 ÷ 9 = _____	72 ÷ 8 = _____
9 x 9 = _____	81 ÷ 9 = _____	81 ÷ 9 = _____

Fold on dotted line. Look above for help.

----

1. Write the multiples of nine (numbers divisible by 9).

9, 18, _____, _____, _____, _____, _____, _____, _____, 90

Each pair of numerals = 9 when added: 1 + 8, 2 + 7, 3 + 6, 4 + 5.

2. x

$3)\overline{}=27$ $9)\overline{45}$ $6)\overline{54}$ $9)\overline{36}$ $8)\overline{72}$ $9)\overline{81}$ $7)\overline{63}$

3.

$9)\overline{18}$ $9)\overline{63}$ $9)\overline{72}$ $4)\overline{36}$ $9)\overline{54}$ $9)\overline{45}$ $9)\overline{27}$

4. You want to buy 45 postcards. They come 9 in a pack. How many packs will you need to buy? _____

5. Next, you want to buy souvenirs for 3 friends. You have $27 left. How much can you spend on each friend? _____

CHALLENGE:
You overheard the park manager say that one fourth of the guests went to the evening show yesterday. If 90 people went to the show, how many guests were at the park? _____

TLC10346 Copyright © Teaching & Learning Company, Carthage, IL 62321-0010

DIVISION–SQUARES & 9s

2 x 9 = ____	2 x 2 = ____	4 ÷ 2 = ____
3 x 9 = ____	3 x 3 = ____	9 ÷ 3 = ____
4 x 9 = ____	4 x 4 = ____	16 ÷ 4 = ____
5 x 9 = ____	5 x 5 = ____	25 ÷ 5 = ____
6 x 9 = ____	6 x 6 = ____	36 ÷ 6 = ____
7 x 9 = ____	7 x 7 = ____	49 ÷ 7 = ____
8 x 9 = ____	8 x 8 = ____	64 ÷ 8 = ____
9 x 9 = ____	9 x 9 = ____	81 ÷ 9 = ____

Fold on dotted line. Look above for help.
- -

1. x 3

$3\overline{)=9}$ $3\overline{)90}$ $30\overline{)90}$ $2\overline{)4}$ $2\overline{)40}$ $20\overline{)40}$

2.

$6\overline{)54}$ $9\overline{)54}$ $9\overline{)540}$ $8\overline{)72}$ $8\overline{)720}$ $9\overline{)720}$

3.

$9\overline{)81}$ $9\overline{)810}$ $90\overline{)810}$ $2\overline{)18}$ $2\overline{)180}$ $90\overline{)180}$

4.

$8\overline{)64}$ $80\overline{)640}$ $80\overline{)720}$ $20\overline{)400}$ $3\overline{)900}$ $70\overline{)630}$

5. Next comes fireworks at Treasure Trove Island. The sign says to thank the 9 sponsors. If fireworks cost a total of $720, how much did each sponsor donate? _____

6. The fireworks took 49 minutes. Each section lasted 7 minutes. How many sections were there? _____

CHALLENGE:
I'm thinking of a number. It's between 20 and 30. It's an even number. If you add the two numerals, you get 8. What is the number? _____

TLC10346 Copyright © Teaching & Learning Company, Carthage, IL 62321-0010

TREASURE TROVE ISLAND

The numbers represent piles of coins on this treasure island. Circle pairs of numbers which total 9. Pairs must be side-by-side, above and below, or diagonal with no other number between.

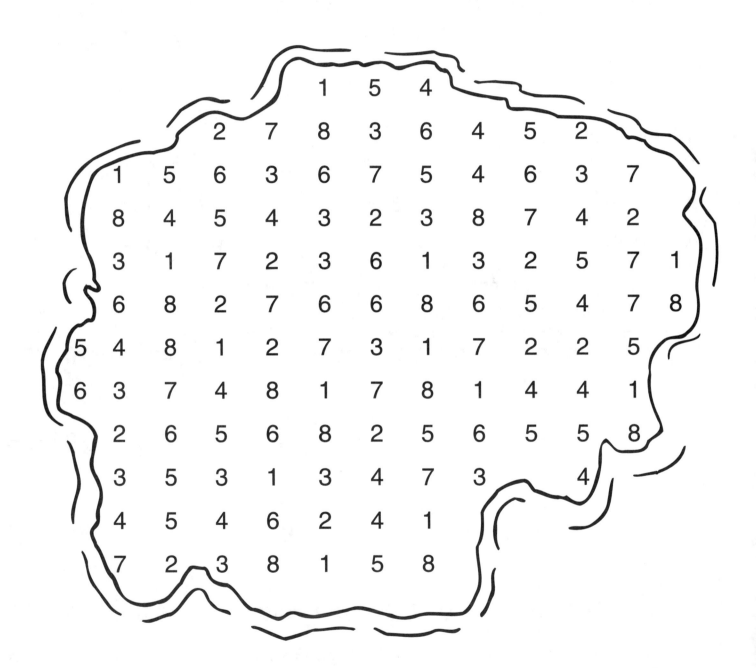

```
              1   5   4
          2   7   8   3   6   4   5   2
    1   5   6   3   6   7   5   4   6   3   7
    8   4   5   4   3   2   3   8   7   4   2
    3   1   7   2   3   6   1   3   2   5   7   1
    6   8   2   7   6   6   8   6   5   4   7   8
5   4   8   1   2   7   3   1   7   2   2   5
6   3   7   4   8   1   7   8   1   4   4   1
    2   6   5   6   8   2   5   6   5   5   8
    3   5   3   1   3   4   7   3       4
    4   5   4   6   2   4   1
    7   2   3   8   1   5   8
```

If a number has numbers totaling nine, that number is divisible by nine.
(Example: 27–2 + 7 = 9 and 27 is divisible by 9.)

TLC10346 Copyright © Teaching & Learning Company, Carthage, IL 62321-0010

OBJECTIVE: Teach or review division with 2, 4 or 8 as the divisor or quotient.

MATERIALS: worksheets (pages 71-75) and mini facts charts (pages 35-36) (optional)

DEMONSTRATION:
Refer to *Math Phonics™–Division*, pages 48-65 as needed.

HANDOUT: Here is a simple classroom game to teach students to predict outcomes and plan strategy. Run off copies of page 76 for student to take home.

The Last Laugh

Each pair of students needs 25 counters such as pennies or buttons. They are called "laughs." If you don't have that many counters, give each student or pair of students a 3" x 5" index card and have them cut it into 25 small rectangles or squares.

Players take turns choosing one, two or three counters. The one to choose last wins. Let students play for a time to see if they can figure out a way that they can always win. Challenge them. Have them play it at home with a sibling or parent. (Winning strategy: If I want to win, I draw first and draw one. This leaves 24 counters. Let the other person draw. No matter what they draw, I draw enough to add up to 4. This always leaves groups of four left. When the last four are left, no matter whether the other person chooses one, two or three, I always can choose last.)

CLASSROOM DRILL: Have the class count by 2s in unison. Then count by 4s in unison, and after sufficient practice, count by 8s. At the top of Worksheet DD (page 74), students should try to see the patterns in the multiples.

WORKSHEETS: For Worksheet BB (page 72), students will check each answer by multiplying the divisor times the quotient. Here is #1:

1.
```
   x    21        21
 4 )=84          x4
      8          84
      4
      4
      0
```

Some problems are with divisors other than 2, 4 or 8, but the answers will be 2s, 4s or 8s.

OPTIONAL: Tell students to make up a rule for when a number is divisible by 2. (If it ends with 0, 2, 4, 6 or 8.)

Tell students to make up a rule for when a number is divisible by 4. (If the number in the 10s place is odd and the number in the 1s place is 2 or 6—12, 16, 32, 36, etc. If the number in the 10s place is even and the number in the 1s place is 0, 4 or 8—20, 24, 28, etc.)

After grading Worksheet AA (page 71), offer extra credit points to any student who will do research and write a brief report about the "pirate" Jean Laffite (pronounced zhäN läfēt´). He was actually a privateer which is slightly different.

After grading Worksheet BB (page 72), give each student a gold "coin"–a foil-covered chocolate candy or foil-covered bubble gum.

Worksheet EE (page 75). Write the answers to all the division problems. Using the answers, connect the dots in order. Students may color a design if they wish.

Worksheet AA (page 71)–Challenge. Many students should be able to solve the post-card challenge on their own. If they need help, show them how to make a grid:

	Island	Pirates	Ocean	Fireworks
Jose	no	yes	no	no
Judy	no	no		
Joan		no		
Julia		no		

When they know for sure that someone did not receive a certain card, they write *no* in that square. (Example: Judy did not get the island.) When they know for sure that someone did get a card, write *yes* in that square. (Example: Jose is the only male so he got the pirates.) Then you can write *no* for Jose getting the other cards and the girls getting the pirate card.

DIVISION-2s

2 x 2 = _____	4 ÷ 2 = _____	4 ÷ 2 = _____
3 x 2 = _____	6 ÷ 2 = _____	6 ÷ 3 = _____
4 x 2 = _____	8 ÷ 2 = _____	8 ÷ 4 = _____
5 x 2 = _____	10 ÷ 2 = _____	10 ÷ 5 = _____
6 x 2 = _____	12 ÷ 2 = _____	12 ÷ 6 = _____
7 x 2 = _____	14 ÷ 2 = _____	14 ÷ 7 = _____
8 x 2 = _____	16 ÷ 2 = _____	16 ÷ 8 = _____
9 x 2 = _____	18 ÷ 2 = _____	18 ÷ 9 = _____

------------------- Fold on dotted line. Look above for help. -------------------

1. x   8
$2\overline{)=16}$ $2\overline{)160}$ $8\overline{)160}$ $3\overline{)6}$ $3\overline{)60}$ $20\overline{)60}$

2.
$2\overline{)4}$ $2\overline{)40}$ $20\overline{)400}$ $5\overline{)10}$ $5\overline{)100}$ $20\overline{)100}$

3.
$9\overline{)18}$ $9\overline{)180}$ $20\overline{)180}$ $2\overline{)14}$ $20\overline{)140}$ $70\overline{)140}$

4.
$4\overline{)80}$ $40\overline{)80}$ $40\overline{)800}$ $6\overline{)12}$ $6\overline{)120}$ $20\overline{)120}$

5. Looking for gold coins at Treasure Trove Island, you have overheard the ranger say that most people find 2 coins each hour. You are hoping to find 14 coins. How many hours will that be? _____

6. People are told to search in pairs. There are 18 people in your tour group. How many pairs will you have? _____

CHALLENGE: You sent postcards to 4 friends—Jose, Judy, Joan and Julia. Their postcards had pictures of 1. the island, 2. pirates, 3. the ocean and 4. fireworks. When you got home, Judy and Julia said they wished they had gotten the island, the person who got fireworks called Julia and Joan to see what was on their cards, and the person who got the pirates said his grandfather looked just like the pirate, Jean Laffite. Who got which cards? _____

Name _____

DIVISION-4s

2 x 4 = _____	8 ÷ 4 = _____	8 ÷ 2 = _____
3 x 4 = _____	12 ÷ 4 = _____	12 ÷ 3 = _____
4 x 4 = _____	16 ÷ 4 = _____	16 ÷ 4 = _____
5 x 4 = _____	20 ÷ 4 = _____	20 ÷ 5 = _____
6 x 4 = _____	24 ÷ 4 = _____	24 ÷ 6 = _____
7 x 4 = _____	28 ÷ 4 = _____	28 ÷ 7 = _____
8 x 4 = _____	32 ÷ 4 = _____	32 ÷ 8 = _____
9 x 4 = _____	36 ÷ 4 = _____	36 ÷ 9 = _____

Fold on dotted line. Look above for help.

- -

Divide and check.

1.
```
   x  21          21
4 )=84         x4
    8          84
    4
    4
    0
```
4)124   9)369   4)168

2.
7)287   4)368   4)132   7)294

3. Treasure Trove Island is open 280 days each year. How many weeks is it open? _____

4. Gold coins found on the island can be sold to a dealer for a price of $4 each. If your group got $168, how many gold coins did the group sell? _____

CHALLENGE:
You have decided each person will choose one gold coin to take home. You roll one die to see who chooses first. You roll first and get a good roll. Your mom rolled a number half as much as yours, and your dad's number was half as much as your mom's. What did each one roll? _____

TLC10346 Copyright © Teaching & Learning Company, Carthage, IL 62321-0010

DIVISION-8s

2 x 8 = _____	16 ÷ 8 = _____	16 ÷ 2 = _____
3 x 8 = _____	24 ÷ 8 = _____	24 ÷ 3 = _____
4 x 8 = _____	32 ÷ 8 = _____	32 ÷ 4 = _____
5 x 8 = _____	40 ÷ 8 = _____	40 ÷ 5 = _____
6 x 8 = _____	48 ÷ 8 = _____	48 ÷ 6 = _____
7 x 8 = _____	56 ÷ 8 = _____	56 ÷ 7 = _____
8 x 8 = _____	64 ÷ 8 = _____	64 ÷ 8 = _____
9 x 8 = _____	72 ÷ 8 = _____	72 ÷ 9 = _____

Fold on dotted line. Look above for help.

- -

Divide and check.

1. $\begin{array}{r} \text{x} \quad 2 \\ 8\overline{)=16} \\ \underline{16} \\ 0 \end{array}$ $\begin{array}{r} 8 \\ \underline{\text{x2}} \\ 16 \end{array}$ $8\overline{)160}$ $5\overline{)405}$ $8\overline{)352}$

2. $8\overline{)416}$ $4\overline{)332}$ $8\overline{)248}$ $8\overline{)576}$

3. $7\overline{)56}$ $7\overline{)581}$ $6\overline{)48}$ $6\overline{)504}$

4. There are about 60 people looking for coins each day. 480 people have signed the new guest book. How many days would that cover? _____

5. The island tram goes about 8 feet per second. How many seconds will it take to go 4800 feet around the island? How many minutes? _____

CHALLENGE:
When the tram circles the island, it makes 5 stops of 8 minutes each. Including the minutes from the last problem, how long will the total trip take? _____

TLC10346 Copyright © Teaching & Learning Company, Carthage, IL 62321-0010

Name _____

2s, 4s & 8s

Write the multiples of 2.

2, _____, _____, _____, _____, _____, _____, _____, _____, **20**

Write the multiples of 4.

4, _____, _____, _____, _____,

_____, _____, _____, _____, **40**

Write the multiples of 8.

8, _____, _____, _____, _____,

_____, _____, _____, _____, **80**

Divide and check.

1.
$$\begin{array}{r} \mathbf{x} \quad 8 \\ 2\overline{)=16} \end{array} \qquad \begin{array}{r} 8 \\ \underline{\times 2} \\ 16 \end{array}$$

$3\overline{)120}$ $90\overline{)180}$ $8\overline{)240}$

2.
$9\overline{)720}$ $80\overline{)160}$ $7\overline{)280}$ $4\overline{)360}$

3.
$$\begin{array}{r} 14 \\ 4\overline{)56} \\ \underline{4} \\ 16 \\ \underline{16} \\ 0 \end{array} \qquad \begin{array}{r} 14 \\ \underline{\times 4} \\ 56 \end{array}$$

$3\overline{)144}$ $6\overline{)144}$ $6\overline{)132}$

4.
$9\overline{)189}$ $4\overline{)172}$ $2\overline{)42}$ $4\overline{)364}$

5.
$8\overline{)176}$ $2\overline{)132}$ $8\overline{)144}$ $2\overline{)198}$

TLC10346 Copyright © Teaching & Learning Company, Carthage, IL 62321-0010

MATH ART

Write all the answers. Using the answers as numbers. Connect the dots in order.

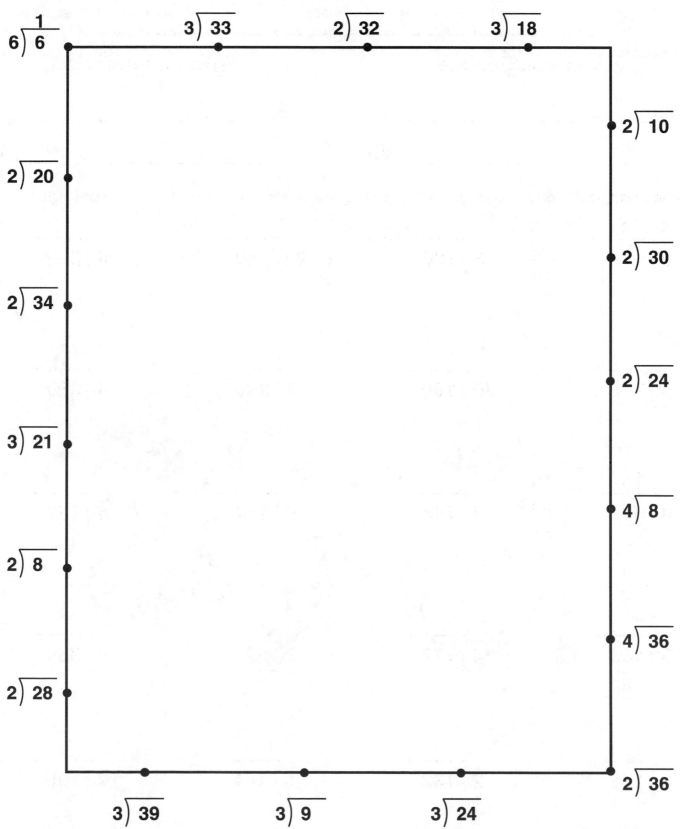

$6\overline{)6}^{1}$

$3\overline{)33}$ $2\overline{)32}$ $3\overline{)18}$

$2\overline{)10}$

$2\overline{)20}$

$2\overline{)30}$

$2\overline{)34}$

$2\overline{)24}$

$3\overline{)21}$

$4\overline{)8}$

$2\overline{)8}$

$4\overline{)36}$

$2\overline{)28}$

$2\overline{)36}$

$3\overline{)39}$ $3\overline{)9}$ $3\overline{)24}$

A lady in your tour group is making a quilt. This is another example of Math Art.

TLC10346 Copyright © Teaching & Learning Company, Carthage, IL 62321-0010

THE LAST LAUGH

A big part of math is thinking ahead, planning how to solve the problem and thinking logically. This game helps to develop all those skills.

The object of the game is to get the last laugh. A laugh is any kind of a counter—a bean, game piece, penny, etc. This should be tried in class until at least some of the students figure it out. Use magnetic tape attached to the back of poker chips if you have a magnetic chalkboard, if not, use 25 sticky notes. Then teach all students the "trick" so they can try it at home or with other friends.

Two-Player Game

Put out 25 counters—or laughs.

Players take turns.

Players may take one, two or three laughs. The winner is the one who takes the last laugh.

TLC10346 Copyright © Teaching & Learning Company, Carthage, IL 62321-0010

OBJECTIVE: Teach or review division with 3s or 6s as the divisor or quotient.

MATERIALS: worksheets (pages 79-80), mini facts charts (pages 35-36) (optional)

DEMONSTRATION: Refer to MPD, pages 76-86 as needed.

Special emphasis on looking at a number and knowing whether it is divisible by 3—very important in reducing fractions—used in algebra and courses above algebra.

HANDOUT: Instructions for "Predict the Answer" (page 78).

CLASSROOM DRILL: Review divisibility rules for 2, 5, 9 and 10. Discuss divisibility by 3 and 6.

If the numerals of a number can be added and will equal 3, 6 or 9, the number can be divided by 3. If it is an even number, it can also be divided by 6.

Examples: 15—1 + 5 = 6 and 15 is divisible by 3.
18—1 + 8 = 9 and 18 is divisible by 3.
18 is also an even number and 18 is divisible by 6.

WORKSHEETS: At the tops of the two worksheets, the division facts are not given. Students should understand how to make a division fact from a multiplication fact. For Worksheet FF, if they are stuck on 22 divided by 3, look at the top of the page. Find the number closest to 22 but still smaller. It is 21. Since 3 x 7 = 21, 3 goes into 22 seven times with 1 remainder.

$$
\begin{array}{r}
7\ \text{r}1 \\
3\overline{)22} \\
\underline{21} \\
1
\end{array}
\qquad
\begin{array}{r}
7 \\
\times 3 \\
\hline
21 \\
+1 \\
\hline
22
\end{array}
$$

If they are having trouble using multiplication facts, have them write the matching division facts first at the top of the page and then do the worksheet.

OPTIONAL: Cooking directions for no-bake cookies: Worksheet FF (page 79). Stir cocoa into sugar. Add milk and butter and heat to boiling. Boil one minute stirring constantly. Immediately add vanilla, and peanut butter and stir. Add oatmeal and stir. Drop by spoonfuls into greased or lined cupcake tins. Each spoonful should be about 3 tablespoons or less as desired. Chill until firm. Enjoy!

PREDICT THE ANSWER

This is a math "trick" you can try on a relative or friend—hereafter referred to as the "victim!" Tell them you are Numero the Great and will predict the sum of 4 numbers they pick, *before they pick them*! Use an old calendar page or Base 10 Counting Chart.

1. Ask the victim to draw a square around 16 numbers anywhere on the calendar or counting chart. The numbers have to all be in a 4 x 4 grid.

2. Glance at the numbers without the person knowing if possible. If you can't sneak a glance, ask to look at the square for one second. Write a number on a piece of paper. Put it where victim can't see it.

3. Tell the person to circle one number anywhere inside the square. Then have the "victim" cross off the other numbers that are in the same line and column.

4. Tell the victim to circle another number—one that has not been circled or crossed off. Then the same to a third number and then a fourth number. By now all the 16 numbers should have been either circled or crossed off.

5. Tell the victim to add the four numbers—but first, you will write the sum of the four numbers on a slip of paper and turn it facedown on the table. Do so.

6. After the victim adds the four circled numbers, turn over the paper you wrote on and show him or her that you were right. If both of you added right, the numbers are the same.

7. What's the trick? When you glance at the paper, look at two numbers in opposite diagonal corners. Add them mentally. Double that sum. This will be the sum of the four circled numbers.

Example: When you look at the square, you see 12 and 45 in opposite diagonal corners.

$$12 + 45 = 57$$

$$57 \times 2 = 114$$

| Step 1 | Step 2 | Step 3 | Step 4 |

Note: This is part of a Base 10 Counting Chart. Numbers would be different on a calendar, but it still works. Have students practice on each other and then try it at home.

TLC10346 Copyright © Teaching & Learning Company, Carthage, IL 62321-0010

DIVISION-3s

3 x 1 = _____	3 x 4 = _____	3 x 7 = _____
3 x 2 = _____	3 x 5 = _____	3 x 8 = _____
3 x 3 = _____	3 x 6 = _____	3 x 9 = _____

Fold on dotted line. Look above for help.

- -

Divide and check.

1. $\begin{array}{r} 8\ r1 \\ 3\overline{)=25} \\ 24 \\ \hline 1 \end{array}$ $\begin{array}{r} 8 \\ \times 3 \\ \hline 24 \\ +1 \\ \hline 25 \end{array}$ $3\overline{)22}$ $3\overline{)28}$ $3\overline{)20}$

2. $40\overline{)126}$ $70\overline{)218}$ $3\overline{)222}$ $30\overline{)284}$

3. $3\overline{)196}$ $3\overline{)77}$ $30\overline{)932}$ $3\overline{)136}$

4. The tour guide has collected money to rent audiotapes about the zoo exhibits. If there is $72, how many $3 tapes can the group rent? _____

5. The zoo cafe sells chocolate drop cookies in groups of 3. There are 96 cookies left in the cupboard. How many plates will be needed for the groups of 3? _____

CHALLENGE:
Here is the recipe for chocolate drop (unbaked) cookies: (T. stands for tablespoon) 32 T. sugar, 4 T. cocoa, 8 T. milk, 12 T. butter, 48 T. oatmeal, 12 T. peanut butter, 8 T. chopped nuts. If each cookie takes 3 T. of batter, how many cookies can be made with one recipe? (There is also I teaspoon of vanilla but don't add that to figure how many cookies.) _____

TLC10346 Copyright © Teaching & Learning Company, Carthage, IL 62321-0010

DIVISION-6s

6 x 1 = _____	6 x 4 = _____	6 x 7 = _____
6 x 2 = _____	6 x 5 = _____	6 x 8 = _____
6 x 3 = _____	6 x 6 = _____	6 x 9 = _____

- - - - - - - - - - - - Fold on dotted line. Look above for help. - - - - - - - - - - - -

Divide and check.

1.

$6\overline{)127}$ $\qquad$ $60\overline{)182}$ $\qquad$ $6\overline{)199}$

2.

$60\overline{)133}$ $\qquad$ $4\overline{)267}$ $\qquad$ $60\overline{)563}$

3.

$90\overline{)550}$ $\qquad$ $60\overline{)493}$ $\qquad$ $6\overline{)385}$

4. The zoo cafe has tables for 6. If the bus holds 48 people, how many tables will your tour group need? _____

5. The zoo hires one person for each 6 animals. If the zoo has 540 animals, how many people need to be hired? _____

CHALLENGE:

What did the zookeeper say about the lion's wounded paw? Work these problems and write each letter above the number of the division answer to read the answer to the question.

E $6\overline{)24}$	H $6\overline{)54}$	I $6\overline{)12}$	R $6\overline{)30}$	W $6\overline{)48}$	N $6\overline{)36}$
T $6\overline{)18}$	A $6\overline{)60}$	S $6\overline{)66}$	O $6\overline{)72}$	P $6\overline{)42}$	

___ ___ ___ ___ ___ ___
8   9   4   6   2   3

___ ___ ___ ___ ___
7   10   2   6   11

___ ___ ___ ___ ___ ___ ___!
2   3   5   12   10   5   11

TLC10346 Copyright © Teaching & Learning Company, Carthage, IL 62321-0010

LESSON PLAN 9: DIVISION FOR 5s & 7s

OBJECTIVE: Teach or review division with 5 or 7 as the divisor or quotient.

MATERIALS: worksheets (pages 83-85) and mini facts charts (pages 35-36) (optional)

DEMONSTRATION:

Refer to *Math Phonics™–Division*, pages 66-75 and 83-86 as needed.

Review multiples of 5 using the Base 10 Counting Chart (page 12) if necessary. Review multiples of 7 using Groups of 7, page 11 in this book. Also, review multiples of 7 using a Base 10 Counting Chart if necessary. Ask for matching division facts for each multiplication fact.

HANDOUT—DIVISOR RACKO: Give each student a set of Racko card pages (pages 86-90) and have them cut them apart. Cards are blank on one side. Here are some ideas for using the cards.

1. Sevens Slapjack. Two-player game. Divide one set of the cards into two piles. Players take turns turning over a card. When a multiple of 7 is turned up, the first one to slap wins all the cards in the pile.

2. Slapjack using any other number. The two players decide on the number.

3. Primes Slapjack. Play the same, but all primes can be slapped. To review primes, see page 88 in *Math Phonics™–Division*.

4. Divisor Racko. Game for two to six players. Also could be used with the entire class divided into two teams. Use one die. Cover the sides with one, four and six spots with a small blank sticker. Write a 3, 9 and 10 on the sides.

   First player rolls the die and draws a card. If the number on the card is divisible by the number on the die, the player must say that it is and give the division fact correctly. Team scores two points.

   If the number on the card is not divisible by the number on the die, divide anyway. Find the remainder and that is the team score. If the number on the card is a prime, the team to yell "prime" first scores 4 points. First team to total 20 points wins.

CLASSROOM DRILL: Use Three-Way Flash Cards to practice division facts.

WORKSHEETS: Practice this group of problems to prepare for Worksheets HH and II (pages 83-84).

$$5 \overline{)35} = 7$$

$$\begin{array}{r} 7 \\ \times 5 \\ \hline 35 \end{array}$$

$$50 \overline{)350} = 7,\ 350,\ 0$$

$$\begin{array}{r} 50 \\ \times 7 \\ \hline 350 \end{array}$$

$$51 \overline{)357} = 7,\ 357,\ 0$$

$$\begin{array}{r} 51 \\ \times 7 \\ \hline 357 \end{array}$$

51 is close to 50 and 357 is close to 350. Think of 35 divided by 5. 7 goes above the 7 in the bracket.

For this problem:

$$49 \overline{)343}$$

49 is close to 50 and 343 is close to 350.

$$50 \overline{)350} = 7$$

$$\begin{array}{r} 50 \\ \times 7 \\ \hline 350 \end{array}$$

Try 7.

$$49 \overline{)343} = 7,\ 343$$

$$\begin{array}{r} 49 \\ \times 7 \\ \hline 343 \end{array}$$

49 is close to 50 and 343 is close to 350, so think of 35 divided by 5. Again, 7 is the guess, and it is the answer.

TLC10346 Copyright © Teaching & Learning Company, Carthage, IL 62321-0010

DIVISION-5s

5 x 1 = _____   5 x 4 = _____   5 x 7 = _____

5 x 2 = _____   5 x 5 = _____   5 x 8 = _____

5 x 3 = _____   5 x 6 = _____   5 x 9 = _____

Fold on dotted line. Look above for help.

Divide and check. Some will have remainders.

1.

$5 \overline{)35}$ $50 \overline{)352}$ $51 \overline{)358}$

2.

$71 \overline{)358}$ $51 \overline{)459}$ $60 \overline{)300}$

3.

$49 \overline{)152}$ $53 \overline{)1613}$ $48 \overline{)578}$

4. The zoo memorial walkway will be made of bricks. If it takes 5 bricks for each square foot, how many square feet can be covered with 1275 bricks? _____

5. Bricks are selling for $70. The tour group took up a collection and raised $280. How many bricks can they buy? _____

CHALLENGE:

Contest at the zoo: The winner gets his or her picture taken riding a camel. The picture will be displayed in the zoo gift shop. The winning number is divisible by 9. It has 2 numerals. If you subtract one numeral from the other, the answer is 1. Your number is 54. Did you win? What other number could win? _____

DIVISION-7s

7 x 1 = _____   7 x 4 = _____   7 x 7 = _____

7 x 2 = _____   7 x 5 = _____   7 x 8 = _____

7 x 3 = _____   7 x 6 = _____   7 x 9 = _____

- - - - - - - - - - Fold on dotted line. Look above for help. - - - - - - - - - -

Divide and check. Some will have remainders

1.

$7 \overline{)56}$ $70 \overline{)560}$ $71 \overline{)570}$

2.

$69 \overline{)280}$ $72 \overline{)1728}$ $73 \overline{)1022}$

3.

$74 \overline{)1554}$ $68 \overline{)612}$ $75 \overline{)153}$

4. The audiotape at the zoo says the elephant's trunk is twice as long as its tail and the body is twice as long as the trunk. If the trunk is 8 feet long, what's the total length from trunk to tail?

_____

5. The mother elephant weighs 7 times as much as the baby elephant. If the mother weighs 791 pounds, how much does the baby weigh? _____

CHALLENGE:

Last day of the trip! Breakfast was great! You realize that you could describe breakfast with 2 letters of the alphabet. What are they? Solve these multiplication problems and write each letter above its answer number in the secret message.

5 x 7 =	5 x 9 =	5 x 5 =	5 x 4 =	5 x 3 =
A	**X**	**N**	**M**	**D**

$\overline{20}$ $\overline{35}$ $\overline{25}$ $\overline{15}$ $\overline{45}$

84

TLC10346 Copyright © Teaching & Learning Company, Carthage, IL 62321-0010

DIVISION–5s & 7s

Think of a math fact related to each problem. Divide and check. Some will have remainders.

1.

$51\overline{)459}$ $71\overline{)639}$ $91\overline{)457}$

2.

$69\overline{)1449}$ $51\overline{)1632}$ $49\overline{)1080}$

3.

$5\overline{)275}$ $51\overline{)255}$ $7\overline{)499}$

4.

$72\overline{)936}$ $50\overline{)361}$ $70\overline{)570}$

5.

$69\overline{)278}$ $50\overline{)407}$ $70\overline{)632}$

6.

$5\overline{)463}$ $7\overline{)578}$ $72\overline{)432}$

1	2	3	4	5
l	Z	E	ъ	ς

6	7	8	9	10
9	L	8	6	01

11	12	13	14	15
11	21	13	14	15

16	17	18	19	20
91	41	81	61	02

TLC10346 Copyright © Teaching & Learning Company, Carthage, IL 62321-0010

21	22	23	24	25
21	22	23	24	25
26	27	28	29	30
26	27	28	29	30
31	32	33	34	35
31	32	33	34	35
36	37	38	39	40
36	37	38	39	40

TLC10346 Copyright © Teaching & Learning Company, Carthage, IL 62321-0010

41	42	43	44	45
41	42	43	44	45
46	47	48	49	50
46	47	48	49	50
51	52	53	54	55
51	52	53	54	55
56	57	58	59	60
56	57	58	59	60

TLC10346 Copyright © Teaching & Learning Company, Carthage, IL 62321-0010

61	62	63	64	65
66	67	68	69	70
71	72	73	74	75
76	77	78	79	80

TLC10346 Copyright © Teaching & Learning Company, Carthage, IL 62321-0010

81	82	83	84	85
81	82	83	84	85
86	87	88	89	90
86	87	88	89	90

90

TLC10346 Copyright © Teaching & Learning Company, Carthage, IL 62321-0010

LESSON PLAN 10: RULES, GAMES & ASSESSMENTS

MULTIPLICATION: See page 85 in *Math Phonics™—Multiplication.*

New Memory Trick:

5 x 5 ends in a 5—25

6 x 6 ends in a 6—36

7 x 7 is a football team—49

8 x 8 fell on the floor.

When they got up, they were 64!

DIVISION: See page 93 in *Math Phonics™—Division* for rules and games.

Games

Multiplication Matchups—page 30
Math Tactics—page 48
The Last Laugh—page 76
Predict the Answer—page 78

Assessments

pages 92-93

For more basic assessments—
page 86 in *Math Phonics™—Multiplication*
page 90 in *Math Phonics™—Division*

TLC10346 Copyright © Teaching & Learning Company, Carthage, IL 62321-0010

MULTIPLICATION

1. 6   4   3   8   4   6   4   7
   x9   x9   x7   x9   x6   x8   x8   x9

2. 7   6   3   4   3   7   6   3
   x8   x7   x6   x5   x9   x7   x6   x4

3. 4   8   6   3   7   8   3   4
   x4   x8   x5   x3   x5   x5   x8   x7

DIVISION

4. 3)12   6)54   8)32   8)40   4)16   3)24   6)30   3)27

5. 8)72   5)35   6)18   6)54   7)63   3)21   4)12   7)28

6. 5)40   4)32   9)27   8)48   7)56   4)24   5)45   8)24

7. 4)20   9)81   6)48   8)56   5)15   3)15   9)72   8)64

8. 3)18   7)42   9)36   4)28   7)49   5)25   7)42   4)36

9. 6)36   9)63   5)30   7)21   6)24   9)45   7)35   8)56

TLC10346 Copyright © Teaching & Learning Company, Carthage, IL 62321-0010

MULTIPLICATION & DIVISION

1. | 50 | 70 | 80 | 400 | 600 | 900 |
    | x2 | x3 | x4 | x3 | x4 | x2 |

2. | 13 | 17 | 24 | 23 | 41 | 34 |
    | x11 | x11 | x11 | x14 | x12 | x13 |

3. | 32 | 18 | 78 | 19 | 47 | 56 |
    | x11 | x32 | x13 | x33 | x21 | x31 |

4. $3\overline{)900}$ $30\overline{)90}$ $6\overline{)360}$ $60\overline{)360}$ $8\overline{)720}$ $9\overline{)540}$

5. $8\overline{)184}$ $3\overline{)123}$ $4\overline{)168}$ $7\overline{)294}$ $8\overline{)256}$ $6\overline{)486}$

Divide. Watch for remainders.

6. $3\overline{)20}$ $4\overline{)126}$ $3\overline{)145}$ $6\overline{)493}$

7. $51\overline{)357}$ $49\overline{)147}$ $71\overline{)568}$

BASE 10 COUNTING CHART

1	2	3	4	5	6	7	8	9	10
11	12	13	14	15	16	17	18	19	20
21	22	23	24	25	26	27	28	29	30
31	32	33	34	35	36	37	38	39	40
41	42	43	44	45	46	47	48	49	50
51	52	53	54	55	56	57	58	59	60
61	62	63	64	65	66	67	68	69	70
71	72	73	74	75	76	77	78	79	80
81	82	83	84	85	86	87	88	89	90
91	92	93	94	95	96	97	98	99	100
101	102	103	104	105	106	107	108	109	110
111	112	113	114	115	116	117	118	119	120
121	122	123	124	125	126	127	128	129	130
131	132	133	134	135	136	137	138	139	140
141	142	143	144	145	146	147	148	149	150

TLC10346 Copyright © Teaching & Learning Company, Carthage, IL 62321-0010

ANSWER KEY

Worksheet A, page 14
Challenge: 452

Worksheet B, page 15
Challenge: 2 days

Worksheet D, page 17

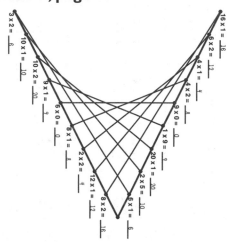

Worksheet E, page 22
Challenge:

14	7	12
9	11	13
10	15	8

Worksheet F, page 23
Challenge: Answers will vary.

Worksheet I, page 38
Challenge: 4

Worksheet J, page 39
Challenge: 456, 465, 564, 546, 645, 654

Worksheet K, page 40
Challenge: VACATION

Worksheet M, page 42

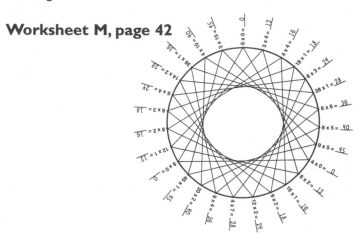

Worksheet O, page 50
Challenge: 9 days

Worksheet P, page 51
1. 0, 7, 14, 21, 28, 35   2. 42, 56, 63, 70, 77, 84
3. 847, 924, 1001, 1078, 1155, 1232   4. 21 candy bars
5. $56.00
Challenge: 13 triangles

Worksheet Q, page 52
1. 8, 16, 24, 32, 40, 48   2. 56, 64, 72, 176, 264, 352
3. 308, 456, 1008, 1856, 1428, 1716   4. $56.00   5. 108 minutes
Challenge:

48	8	64
56	40	24
16	72	32

Worksheet R, page 60
1. 30, 9, 35, 40, 24, 28   2. 64, 16, 12, 36, 49, 27
3. 32, 63, 20, 18, 42, 56   4. 54, 36, 72, 24, 21, 48
5. 420, 810, 480, 2500, 5600, 1500   6. 52, 111, 132, 231, 176, 264
7. 432, 517, 696, 1116, 1533, 1848

Worksheet S, page 60
Challenge: $ 2.4⃞0⃞
                 1.⃞7⃞8
             +⃞3⃞.25
               $ 7.43

Worksheet T, page 61
Challenge: It's in the middle of fun!

Worksheet U, page 62
Challenge:

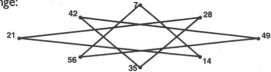

Worksheet V, page 63
Challenge: 100, 200, 600, 6000
Rule: Multiply the non-zero numbers. Add one zero for each zero in the problem.

Worksheet W, page 64

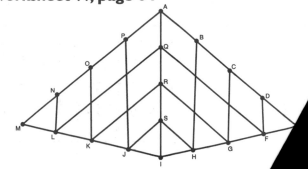

TLC10346 Copyright © Teaching & Learning Company, Carthage, IL 62321-0010

ANSWER KEY

Worksheet X, page 66
Challenge: 360 guests

Worksheet Y, page 67
1. 30, 3, 2, 20, 2   2. 9, 6, 60, 9, 90, 80   3. 9, 90, 9, 9, 90, 2
4. 8, 8, 9, 20, 300, 9   5. $80.00   6. 7 sections
Challenge: 26

Worksheet Z, page 68

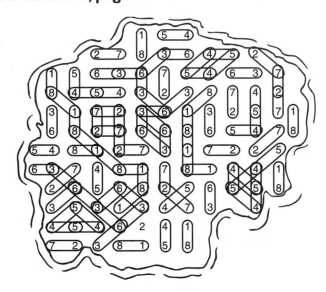

Worksheet AA, page 71
1. 80, 20, 2, 20, 2   2. 2, 20, 20, 2, 20, 5   3. 2, 20, 9, 7, 7, 2
4. 20, 2, 20, 2, 20, 6   5. 7 hrs.   6. 9 pairs
Challenge: Jose got Pirates, Judy got fireworks, Joan got the island and Julia got the ocean.

Worksheet BB, page 72
1. 31, 41, 42   2. 41, 92, 33, 42   3. 40 weeks   4. 42 coins
Challenge: You rolled 4; Mom rolled a 2; Dad rolled 1

Worksheet CC, page 73
1. 20, 41, 44   2. 52, 88, 31, 72   3. 8, 83, 8, 84
4. 8 days   5. 600 seconds (10 minutes)
Challenge: 50 minutes

Worksheet DD, page 74
1. 40, 2, 30   2. 80, 20, 40, 90   3. 48, 24, 22
?1, 43, 21, 91   5. 42, 32, 83, 81   6. 22, 66, 18, 99

Worksheet EE, page 75

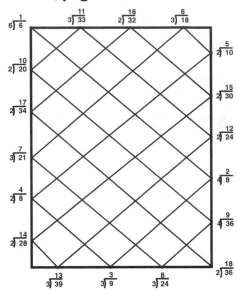

Worksheet FF, page 79
1. 7r1, 9r1, 6r2   2. 3r6, 3r8, 74, 9r14   3. 65r1, 25r2, 31r2, 45r1
4. 24 tapes   5. 32 plates
Challenge: 41 cookies with 1 T. left over.

Worksheet GG, page 80
1. 21r1, 3r2, 33r1   2. 2r13, 66r3, 9r23   3. 6r10, 8r13, 64r1
4. 8 tables   5. 90 people
Challenge: When it pains, it roars! (Spoonerism for when it rains, it pours.) W.A. Spooner was a minister of New College, Oxford, famous for slips of the tongue.

Worksheet HH, page 83
1. 7, 7r2, 7r1   2. 5r3, 9, 5   3. 3r5, 30r23, 12r2
4. 255 square feet   5. 4 bricks
Challenge: yes; 45

Worksheet II, page 84
1. 8, 8, 8r2   2. 4r4, 24, 14   3. 21r32, 9, 2r3
4. 28 feet   5. 113 pounds
Challenge: M and X (ham and eggs)

Worksheet JJ, page 85
1. 9, 9, 5r2   2. 21, 32, 22r2   3. 55, 5, 71r2
4. 13, 7r11, 8r10   5. 4r2, 8r7, 9r2   6. 92r3, 82r4, 6

Assessment, page 93
1. 100, 210, 320, 1200, 2400, 1800
2. 143, 187, 264, 322, 492, 442
3. 352, 576, 1014, 627, 987, 1736
4. 300, 3, 60, 6, 90, 60
5. 23, 41, 42, 42, 32, 81
6. 6r2, 31r2, 48r1, 82r1
7. 7, 3, 8

TLC10346 Copyright © Teaching & Learning Company, Carthage, IL 62321-0010